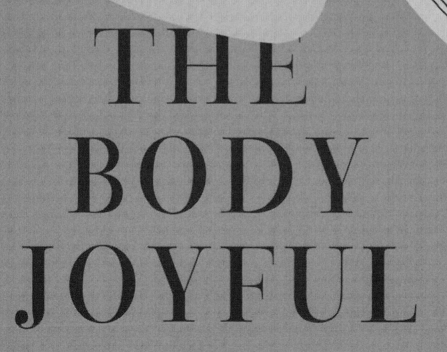

My journey from
self-loathing to
self-acceptance

THE
BODY
JOYFUL

ANNE POIRIER

ENDORSEMENTS

"Sometimes reading someone else's story can be a great illuminator to the struggles that we are facing internally. Anne Poirier's book, *The Body Joyful,* does just that. A helpful book for someone who wants to start their body-positive journey with the added bonus of interesting reflection questions to round up the chapters."

—**Connie Sobczak,** Co-Founder and Executive Director of The Body Positive and author of *Embody: Learning to Love Your Unique Body (and quiet that critical voice)*

"The key to flourishing—regardless of your curent weight or size--is to feel joy. Every system in the female body works best in this state—including the endocrine system, the immune system, and the central nervous system. The problem is that society has tried to put women in an actual or imagined "corset" of ideals that few women can attain. This leads to a lifetime of dieting, self-denial, and self-abnegation that can go on for decades. But you can break out of that corset in a heartbeat. Annie Poirier lays out the path in *The Body Joyful.*"

—**Christiane Northrup, M.D.,** *New York Times best-selling author of Goddesses Never Age, The Wisdom of Menopause, and Women's Bodies, Women's Wisdom*

"This inspiring, motivational book will help you unlock your self-confidence and feel wonderful about yourself. You learn that you have no limits!"

—**Brian Tracy,** Author/Speaker/Consultant

"*The Body Joyful* is exactly what the doctor ordered to combat the lies that we as women feed ourselves. Whether these lies have come from diet culture or your past "seeds" as Anne calls them, she speaks directly to your soul. As someone who has struggled with body image and a poor relationship with food, this book was for me. Anne is relatable, clever, and honest. I literally didn't want to stop reading and I have a feeling whomever reads this book won't want to stop either. Thank you, Anne for sharing this gem with the world!"

—**Achea Redd,** Author of *Be Free Be You* and *Authentic You,*
Founder of blog Real Girls F.A.R.T.

"Anne takes you on a journey that is powerful and moving. If you, or a daughter, sister, or friend has ever struggled with food, or felt like you weren't enough, this book will be an inspiration and a path forward. Anne is the voice for the anti-diet movement!"

—**Pamela Bruner,** *Author, Business Owner*

"For anyone who cringes at the words 'weight loss,' 'eating disorder,' or 'body shame,' reading Body Joyful will prove a welcome sigh of relief that someone finally gets you. Anne Poirier selflessly shares her dysfunctional journey with weight and body image, giving you permission and tools to break up your own relationship that isn't working. I am excited to use this book as a tool in my psychotherapy practice."

—**Dr. Zoe Shaw,** Redefining your superwoman podcast

THE
BODY
JOYFUL

*My journey from self-loathing
to self-acceptance*

ANNE POIRIER

WOODHALL PRESS
NORWALK, CT

Woodhall Press, 81 Old Saugatuck Road, Norwalk, CT 06855
WoodhallPress.com

Cover design: Asha Hossain
Layout artist: Sheryl Kober

Library of Congress Cataloging-in-Publication Data available
ISBN 978-1-949116-81-6 (paper: alk paper)
ISBN 978-1-949116-82-3 (electronic)
First Edition
Distributed by Independent Publishers Group
(800) 888-4741
Printed in the United States of America

DISCLAIMER
Trigger Warning: [Food, ED, MH]
During the writing of my story, I tried to follow the NEDA (National Eating Disorders Association) guidelines for media. Yet, there are stories with details of disturbed and disordered thoughts, beliefs and behaviors around food, binging, restricting, overexercising, drinking, and more. If any of my stories or words trigger you into feeling like dieting, binging, restricting, not eating, fasting, overeating, or other addictive, compulsive-type behavior, please seek help. Call the toll-free NEDA helpline at 1-800-931-2237 9 a.m.-9 p.m. For 24/7 crisis support via text NEDA at 741-741.

For my Mom and Dad, Pat and Chuck.

The only way this book is written is because of the two of you and the life we shared as parents and child. This kind of relationship does not need genetic ties; it just needs consistent, durable, deep-seated love. The type I needed and the type you both provided. Thank you for choosing me, supporting me, encouraging me, and bringing me home to you. Words cannot express the gratitude and love I have ingrained in my heart for you both. Sending a heart to heaven aimed straight for you, Mom.
I know you will catch it.

Contents

Introduction

I stand naked in front of the full-length mirror in the dressing room. Something familiar bubbles up from the knot in my stomach. Captain Criticism and her team begin to rally. The shame storm, judgment jury, and blame board are gathered in the corner of my brain. They know exactly where to look and what to say to make sure they are heard loud and clear by me.

I fight the tears and turn my back to the mirror. I take a deep breath and recruit my inner Maxi-Me. (Maxi-Me is my strong, compassionate, kind, and empowering inner voice whom I have created to help me fight the others.) I need you, right here, right now. I don't want to keep playing this role and living this story. Help me to start writing a different story for myself. It has been too long, and I am too tired to keep up this fight.

What have you got to say for yourself, Maxi???

I take another deep breath, pause, and turn around to face the judge once again. In front of me I see a fifty-six-year-old woman who has been imprisoned by her own perspectives. She has worn a single pair of glasses since birth. These glasses have clouded her vision, colored her view, and blurred the truth of who she truly is.

It started with the belief that I didn't look or feel like the other kids. I was bigger, boxier, and clumsier, more curious and tenacious. I didn't care about makeup, dolls, boys, and dresses. I didn't want to read, play house, or watch cartoons. I didn't care about anything my family or classmates wanted to do either. I cared about climbing trees, playing catch, and hopping on my pogo stick. I wanted to explore the backwoods and catch pollywogs in the pond across the street. No one else in our neighborhood liked these things, leaving me wondering what was wrong with me.

It left me feeling alone, abandoned, and then addicted. It led me to use food, eating, and exercise to numb out. It led me to behaviors that I am ashamed of and embarrassed by. I have drunk too much, kept secrets, and told lies. I've snuck in binges and work-outs and diets and sex…all to try to disappear within myself. It's been a way of "showing myself" I was not worthy. A way of proving to myself I deserve to be abandoned and dismissed.

A continuous running toward and away from myself. Restricting, binging, drinking, running, pushing, striving, searching. Never feeling good enough or fitting in anywhere, nothing I did was ever quite right.

This is the story about the how and why I landed in a deep, dark hole, stayed there for forty years, and how I made the decision to climb out. It is about the thoughts and voices in my head that have dictated my actions, behaviors, and choices. On this journey my own thoughts were the shovel that dug my hole deeper. My internal voices and perspectives proceeded to throw me into it. These perspectives placed a door and lock on top of the hole, keeping me held prisoner deep inside. This is the story of my escape from the prison of my own perspective.

The experiences I had in childhood planted seeds inside of me that birthed my beliefs. These beliefs then flourished and became stronger as I grew older. The seeds are made of simple experiences. Much like having a parent ask you to change your shirt, because the stripes are going the wrong way. *"When you wear horizontal stripes, it makes you look fat,"* they would say.

Once a seed like this is planted in our brain, it becomes a magnet to notice similar words, thoughts, and experiences. When this happens, we make assumptions and place precious energy and attention to whatever it is we think about ourselves. Our brain is now programmed to continue to be on the lookout to prove the thoughts we have about ourselves. These perspectives (thoughts and beliefs) feel like truths. They strengthen our identities and the stories we live in.

It works like this: You decide you want to buy a red truck for your next vehicle. As soon as your decision is made, your attention is now more aware and focused on looking at red trucks. You have enlisted your brain to help you out.

These seeds can be planted around your looks and appearance. They can be planted around mannerisms, opinions, words, and choices. These seeds become your story, your identity, and how you think of yourself. Once planted, your brain has accepted the mission to find proof. It looks for more red trucks.

This book shares my brain's search for the "red trucks" of thought that were planted in me as a child. It also opens the door for you, if you choose, to see what red trucks you might be holding on to. As you read, you may…

1. Notice feelings that come up in your body.
   a. When you feel something in your body, it's a sign to take notice. It's like an annoying little sister (or brother) who continues to tap you on the shoulder until you turn to notice them. These feelings can be subtle, so listen close and give yourself permission to explore them.

   b. If you feel tightening or tension in your body, it may be a sign there is something familiar about what you are reading. It can feel heavy, like you've been carrying around a weight that may need some unpacking.

   c. If you feel a lightness or an excitement around something you read, it's a sign to take out a journal and jot down what is coming up for you. Lightness, excitement, and joy are wonderful signs to pay attention to. They're asking you to look up.

If you choose, you can take the time to answer the questions at the end of most chapters. They are designed to allow you the space and time to see your life from a different perspective.

If you choose to just read or skip over the questions in this book, it may become just another book on your shelf. Taking the time to be curious can make this book a catalyst for change.

As you read, have compassion and kindness for yourself. This can be a foreign concept to many. Do you put yourself down, judge, or criticize yourself? Think about the way you have been talking to yourself so far in your life. How has that been working for you? This might be a great time for a curious experiment of trying a new compassionate voice:

a. Become aware of the words, phrases, and tone of voice you use inside your head. You can only change something once you become aware of it.

b. Imagine hearing your own harsh, critical negative thoughts for a moment. Think about if you were hearing them coming out of the mouth of a five-year-old you. What might you say in response to him or her?

What tone of voice, what words, what actions might you use? This is compassion.

As you read my story, feel free to be open to your own voices, beliefs, and perspectives. Explore, question, and to be curious. And then curiously challenge your thoughts, your beliefs, and your story.

PART I
PLANTING

"You're a human being, you live once and life is wonderful,
so eat the damn red velvet cupcake."

—Emma Stone

CHAPTER 1

Brownies

OCTOBER 1979. PRACTICE WAS CANCELLED SO I FOUND MYSELF home alone early from school. My stomach was growling, and I hadn't eaten for hours. I am standing alone in the kitchen, counting and calculating my day. How many calories have I eaten today? I want something to eat, no one will know. *Yes, NO, Yes, NO...* the voices in my head fight with each other. *Don't blow it, you have been so good. Maybe I'll make something for the family? Yes! That's it, that would be good, then I can at least smell it.*

I open and close the cabinet doors seeking and searching for something. Suddenly, I remember the beautiful red Duncan Hines brownie box I saw my mom unpack the other day.

Where is it? It has to be here somewhere. Frantically, I move cans, push boxes out of the way, and keep searching. Bingo. There it is, that alluring red Duncan Hines brownie box. *Yes!* I will make brownies for the family.

I grab it, forage for the ingredients, pull out a bowl, turn on the oven, and dig for a pan. Mix, egg, oil, water, mix. I am on automatic, like a possessed robot. Step by step on fast forward. My mind is telling me this will be just for the family. This will be great! I won't have any of it. They will eat all the calories. I will just make it.

I throw the pan in the oven and set the timer. Wash the bowl and spoon before I ruin everything by taking a bite of the batter. I keep repeating *no, no, no, don't eat any, please don't eat any.* The words were quickly followed by commentary from my Mini-Me voice. *You are a fat pig, you can't have any of these, these are not for you, you don't deserve to eat any of them.*

I run upstairs and lie on the floor and start doing my sit-ups, Mini-Me taunting me that I have gained weight and that I have to start controlling myself...One, two, three...

The buzzer sounds. I run downstairs and pull the brownies out. My stomach still hurts and is growling, my head is fuzzy, my mouth is watering. *Just one bite, just one, just one.* The words circle around in my head. *One won't hurt, then I will say I am not feeling well for dinner and not eat anything.*

I cut a thin sliver down one end...I love the edges of the brownie, that's my favorite part. Before I even know what happened the whole strip of that side of the pan is in my mouth. In my belly and tasted so good. *That is soooo good, just a little more, just one more bite....*

The next time I look down, the pan is empty. I have just eaten a whole pan of brownies. *Shit.* My heart starts to race and feels like it is beating out of my chest. I start to sweat, feeling both humiliated and horrified with myself. How the heck did this happen?

It was like I blacked out. *I am such a loser...I can't do anything right. Mom is going to kill me, there are no brownies for any of them and the box is gone. What am I going to do?* I start to panic, and I don't know where to turn. My head is spinning. I look at my watch, 3:45. There is enough time. I run up into my room and dig in the drawers in search of some money. *I have to, they can't find out. I can do this. I have time to get to the store to get another box.*

I scrape the remaining crumbs of brownie into a bag followed by the box. Out the door I run with the bag clenched tightly in my hand. I hop on my bike and take off to the store. I had it all planned out. I will get rid of the evidence of my failure. My feet pedal faster as the bag swings back and forth on the handlebars, a constant reminder of what I had done. I throw away the bag in the trash outside the store and get the goods. A replacement red Duncan Hines brownie box. Within minutes I am back on my bike and pedaling home as fast as I can.

I speed up the driveway and ditch my bike all in one motion behind the garage, grab the goods, and run into the house. The oven is still on, the freshly washed bowl is still in the sink rack. All the ingredients are still out on the counter...measure, mix, bake. Get the brownies done. *Faster, Anne, faster!*

In the oven they go, 4:40. Done. They will be out by the time my mother gets home. I breathe a sigh of relief. I spin around the kitchen, making sure all the evidence is gone. Dishes done, ingredients put away, no brownie crumbs to be seen.

I sit down, relieved and calm, and smile. No one will ever know! *I got away with it! A* wave of satisfaction washes over me. I ate brownies and my parents will never know. *I am victorious!*

This calmness lasts mere seconds because the voice and vision rush back into my mind. There it is, the empty brownie pan. I ate a whole pan of brownies…

Without missing a beat, the shame storm starts to swirl in my head. Mini-Me starts her assault with her harsh, angry, sarcastic tone. Beating me up, judging, criticizing and degrading me. My relentless Mini-Me rears her ugly head. *You are such a loser, you will never be able to control yourself, how many calories did you just eat? Everyone is going to know you pigged out, they will see it in how tight your clothes are tomorrow. You are so stupid…such a pig, why can't you control yourself around food? Why are you always doing this? You are always going to be fat; no one is ever going to like you. I hate you so much.*

The tears stream down my face. I get down onto the floor, right there in the dining room, and start my punishment…one, two, three.

August 2020

I just finished reading this brownie story to a small group of strangers. When I look up, there are tears in their eyes and a silent stillness that is almost spooky. The word "shit" sits in my brain. Uh-oh, this could be bad. A woman breaks the silence: "I could have written that myself," and others nod their heads. I am not alone. They are not alone.

"Do you eat brownies now?" another asks.

"Yes, as a matter of fact," I say with a smile, "I have a Duncan Hines brownie box sitting at home waiting for me to bake when I am done here." Brownies are no longer the enemy; neither is my Mini-Me. The strangers don't feel like strangers anymore. They feel like friends. There is a quiet, common connection between us all. And, because I have shared this story, they hear healing, see happy, and feel hopeful.

CHAPTER 2

Seeds

IT'S JANUARY 1964. A FOUR-MONTH-OLD BABY WITH JET-BLACK hair, alone in a crib, just spit up all over herself. A tall, thin man in a black suit and a petite woman wearing a tan cardigan sweater walk in. They take one look at this chubby little baby girl and say, "We'll take her." The woman wants to take her home to clean her up and the man's heart has just broken wide open. These people have just decided to become my parents.

Four months earlier, a sixteen-year-old girl gave birth to me. She was alone somewhere near Boston. I would imagine she was anxious, confused, and frightened. This teenager was my birth mother. I know nothing about her. And yet I am grateful. Being a pregnant teen in 1963 couldn't have been easy.

From the afternoon in early October to that day in January, my whereabouts are unknown. It is unknown who held me, who fed me, or who changed my diaper. All I remember was being known as a "chubby little baby."

Chubby was how my parents described me. Lots of babies are chubby. Yet for me, that was the start of the belief that I was fat. My dad called me a butterball, my mom called me stocky and sturdy, they both called me a bull in a china shop. You know...a bull, the big fat animal that always knocks things down and bumps into things. Unfortunately, I interpreted these words differently than they were expressed. They thought cute, energetic, and spirited; I thought fat, clumsy, and stupid. Seeds planted by my own interpretation.

These two people, the ones I call my mom and dad, chose to take me home and make me part of their family. They taught me to be kind to other people and to work hard. My mom had a quick wit and contagious smile. She was extremely artistic and organized. Our weekly dinners were posted on the fridge every week of my childhood. A habit she continued well into her eighties. My dad was an electrical engineer. Very smart, dedicated, and hardworking. He had high expectations of himself and perfectionistic tendencies too. It was rare to see him *not* involved in some committee, project, or activity. He was always looking for something to sink his teeth into.

We grew up in a privileged, white, middle-class home in a small North Shore town in Massachusetts. My parents shared their beliefs and thoughts on religion, politics, money, and education. They also shared the truth of what they deemed to be a healthy body size. They shared their expectations around success and failure and how they expected us to behave. To say please and thank you. To be polite and put together.

The Planting of Seeds

For me, my beliefs and identity formed around the words people said to me or to my parents. Phrases like "What a chubby little child." "Look at those chubby little cheeks." "Wow, she's big for a girl." "Your thighs are huge!" "Why don't you pay attention?" "Geez, you have your hands full!" "Anne, watch where you are going!"

The birth of stupid, fat, clumsy, and "I am not good enough" come from these simple conversations. They come from memories of me running up the stairs to my bedroom and flopping on my bed sobbing to myself, *I can't do anything right. I am always messing up, I'm so stupid...or fat... or clumsy.*

The seeds of these early years planted a hatred inside of me, a hatred of myself. It was from this hatred a deep desire of wanting to be "liked and accepted" grew. It encouraged me to find a way to change myself to get others to like me.

I went on a quest to find proof I was OK. All I wanted was to fit in, because I knew that if I did, I would be happy.

The seeds became the birthplace of the beliefs I held on to and carried with me into adulthood. My first identities, planted from the words I heard, over and over again. Many of these voices have made themselves at home in my head. They live in a neighborhood there. I took them in and held on to them as my own. I have named these negative voices my Mini-Me's. I will introduce you as we go...

The Clumsy Seed

Crash went the chair to the ground as I ran around the corner of the dining room into the kitchen. I stopped dead in my tracks. I stood in front of my mother with her hands on her hips, "Watch what you're doing, Anne, inside is no place for running. Go run outside if you want to run."

Fair enough, that made sense to my five-year-old brain, so out the front door I went. I started to run around the house. I quickly took off running. Up the hill on one side, around the back porch and down the hill on the other side. My arms stretched out to my side as if I was an airplane. "Zooommmmm," I yelled as I passed my dad on a ladder painting our yellow house a dark shade of brown.

"Slow down and watch out for that paint can," he stated from the top of the ladder.

I was in my own world. I loved the feeling of the wind in my hair, especially as I ran down the hill. I skipped, walked, and galloped around the house again until I ran down the hill once again... "Slow down and watch out for that paint can! Anne," my dad repeated yet again.

"I know, I see it." I yelled up, annoyed.

Round and round I went, each time, my father telling me to watch out for the paint can...*ya, ya, ya...*

Crash, smack, oops! Right into the paint can I went, the paint went everywhere. All over me, all over the ladder, the house, and all the ground.

"ANNE! What have I been telling you? You have to watch where you are going. You are like a bull in a china shop. Please start paying attention." His voice was sharp and disappointed. I know this voice, I think to myself. I have disappointed him again.

This type of behavior was second nature for me. I grew up falling all the time. Banging my head on cabinet doors, tripping over stumps, and bumping into coffee tables. I would jump and miss and end up breaking things and breaking me. I could be looking one way only to run into something right in front of me.

Because of these words, memories, and experiences, I know I am clumsy. It has been ingrained in my subconscious and consciousness. I am just plain klutzy. I don't pay attention. I don't watch what I am doing and get lost in my active mind that is running its own race a mile a minute. This has become my story.

Even today, when I stub my toe, hit my hip on the counter or my head on the cabinet door, the voice in my head just sighs and says, "why don't you start watching what you are doing, you are such a klutz" or "you are so stupid, why don't you pay attention." Anything that is perceived as even remotely clumsy has become "who I am."

When I break something, my inner voice chimes in. It attaches to the old thoughts and beliefs I hold tight too, my Mini-Me. She ramps up to say, *"You are so clumsy. You are always doing things like this. Why do you always try to do so many things at once! When will you learn? You are such a loser; you can't do anything right."* She gets louder and louder, meaner and meaner, as if to make sure I hear the confirmation of the so-called *truth* of who I am.

The *"I am clumsy and don't pay attention"* seed has been deeply rooted into my brain.

The Messy Seed

YAY, I get to go to school! I was SO excited to be going to kindergarten class! I had watched my brother leave every day to go to "school." I saw how proud and happy my parents were when he left to catch the bus every day. And how excited they were to talk to him about his day when he came home.

I couldn't wait to start; *this school thing must be amazing!*

I skipped into my kindergarten room as happy as a clam. Mrs. G, my kindergarten teacher, looked like a grandma. She was greeting all the kids, wearing a long blue skirt, light pink shirt, and had short gray hair. She spoke with a gentle but stern tone, trying her best to control a classroom that was filling up with high-energy five-year-olds. The classroom had a small reading corner with a carpet, where Mrs. G. would read to us, easels set up on one full side of the room for art, and small tables in the middle where we would make puzzles and learn our letters. This kindergarten thing was going to be amazing.

The second week of school Mrs. G gave me a note to bring home to my mom. *Wow, none of the other kids have a note to bring home. My brother never brought a note home! I must be doing so good! Yay for me!* I was so very proud to be bringing that note home. I knew I must be doing something right!

Excitedly, I ran in the house. "Mom!" I yelled. She emerged from the dining room dressed in her lilac sweatsuit. The one she wore whenever she exercised. I held up the note to her.

She smiled, opened it, and began to read out loud because she could see how excited I was. She became puzzled as she read, thinking maybe she should have read it to herself…

Dear Mrs. Poirier,

I am writing to inform you that Anne is no longer allowed to finger-paint or take part in art class with us. She is too messy and is a distraction to all the other children. Her art station is always a mess and today she had paint all over herself, the floor, and the other students. Please let her know, she will be sitting out during art from now on.

Thank you,
Mrs. G.

I saw the disappointment in my mom's face. I was confused and sad and didn't understand.

My mom sat down on the couch and asked me to sit next to her so she could explain. With a gentle voice she let me know I wouldn't get to take part in art class anymore. She proceeded to tell me, "Sometimes you get too excited, and you don't watch what you're doing." And "You can be a bit clumsy and messy."

Another seed planted in my five-year-old brain.

Seeds of Belief

These seeds took root and became deeper and deeper beliefs. Once they started to grow, it was easy to keep proving it to myself over and over and over again. As I continued to have experiences, the beliefs grew stronger. They took on new meanings too. Thoughts and beliefs like *I'm not creative, I'm scattered, unfocused, uncoordinated.*

It is easy to find proof of the belief because the thought was already there. I think of it like a magnetic field. One small spill of milk floods into an onslaught of negative self-talk. The one thought, *I am so clumsy*, gets connected to *I am always making a mess.* Which then connects to *I shouldn't even be allowed to pour milk.* Which then connects to *how stupid am I that I thought I could do that anyway.*

Years and years of more and more experiences prove to me that I am clumsy and messy.

And of course, I am not done planting yet…

Planting the Stupid Seed

The stupid seed was planted firmly in first grade. I had a small group of friends and there were a couple girls who would play with me at recess. One day, a popular classmate (let's call her Martha) wanted to come over to my house to play. She begged and begged me. So, I asked my mother if she could, and my mom promptly said no.

I sulked and asked why…and her response was a simple "Because I said so."

This answer did not satisfy me at all and placed an uncomfortable feeling in my stomach like I wanted to throw up. I was sad and angry at my mom. All the other girls liked Martha and hung around her and she was asking *me* to be her friend.

I didn't need my mom's permission, I thought. All I needed was a note to give my teacher to let her come home with me. *Great plan, Anne,* I thought. Off I went to secretly borrow my mom's special "note-making" notepad. I wrote a note to my teacher (Mrs. R.) from my mother: *Martha is able to go home on bus 6 with Anne today.* I then proceeded to sign it, *Mrs. Poirier.* I carefully put my mother's notepad back in its special spot on her desk.

I was so proud of my note and so happy that Martha was going to come over to play. I would actually have a friend to play with after school. The morning passed by without a word from my teacher. *I did it!* I thought.

When Mrs. R. called us all to line up at the front door for lunch, I could see she had something in her hand. As we all assembled, she said she had an announcement to make. Right in front of the room, she held up MY NOTE in broad daylight for the whole class to see. I stood in shock while she lectured me.

"Anne has written a note and signed her mother's name to it. This is called forgery and is against the law." She proceeded to let me and the class know she wasn't stupid and that I was stupid for thinking I could get away with this. She continued on, "At least if you were going to forge a note, Anne, you would want to make sure that you spelled all the words correctly!"

She then used my note as an example to the other kids in the class. She showed them how I transposed my b's and d's, making some of the words misspelled. "Let this be a lesson for all of you. This is a dishonest, sneaky, and deceitful act, and shows bad judgment."

Needless to say, Martha wanted nothing to do with me after that. This was the birthplace of Stupid Sally; she was born in that first-grade lunch line. A loud critical voice in my head who made sure I knew every time I did something wrong. She would pop into my head anytime I did something clumsy, dishonest, sneaky, or stupid. A new belief was born. I am stupid. I also started to believe I was different from all the other kids. I just didn't seem to fit in anywhere.

The seeds of these early years sprouted into individual voices in my head. Thus, they became my earliest identities. The Mini-Me voices included Stupid Sally and Clumsy Carla. You are stupid, you're clumsy, you're messy, and you don't fit in.

Taking a Step Back

As you move through this book, you will notice "Step Backs" at the end of most chapters. Step Backs are a few questions you have the opportunity to ask yourself.

The Step Back is just that. It is taking a step back to widen the vision on the whole situation you are thinking about. Who else is involved? What might they be thinking? Where are you? What may have happened earlier in the day? The step backs are a way to see a different perspective of a particular experience, thought, or feeling.

Here are a few ways you can use them:

- You can read the book with a journal, stopping at each Step Back and diving into the questions. This allows you the space and time to take a closer look at the way your own life has been sculpted. And begin to identify who you think you are and what you believe.

- You can read the book without reading the Step Backs. Then come back to them after you're done to ponder your own perspectives with curiosity.

- You can read the book and the Step Backs and pick certain ones to do and other ones to skip.

Your choice. There is no right or wrong way. Choose the way you want to move through this journey for yourself.

Step Back

The bigger picture:

1. Identify some "seeds" of your own. Where did they come from? Who was involved?

2. What is the earliest memory you can link to an identity you hold on to?

3. How do these beliefs impact how you think, act, and behave today?

CHAPTER 3

Husky

The Biggest Seed

I ran down the stairs and out the front door, hearing it slam behind me. The boys were in the backyard playing football and I wanted to play. I tore around the house toward the backyard. I couldn't wait to get out there.

I am going to play football with my brother. My brother was adopted too, two years earlier than me. We actually share the same birthday, weird but true. In my eyes, I saw him as tall and thin, blond and smart, creative and popular. I wanted to get his attention, for him to see me and notice me. If he did, I would be happy. *He will let me play; he has to let me play…I am his sister. I can't wait to show him how strong I am, how good I can be. He will want me on his team…*

Up the hill I sprinted toward the back field next door. It was a large field, perfect for us kids to play on. Two large oak trees marked the sidelines when the boys played soccer or football, and those same trees separated the infield from the outfield in baseball or kickball when you turned the field the other way.

"Hi, can I play?" I yelled as soon as I got close enough.

"Hey look!" one of the boys yelled. "It's Annie Fannie Farmer, coming to ask us to play."

The boys turned, all six of them and they started to chant: "*Annie Fannie Farmer, Annie Fannie Farmer, Annie Fannie Farmer.*" It was a taunting rhythm that stopped me in my tracks. The words caught me off guard. *What? What are they saying?*

I stood there, staring at my brother with hope. Wanting him to say or do something. He fit in with his friends. He wasn't clumsy like me, wasn't messy like me, didn't look different than the other kids. He was normal. I wanted to be normal too.

The boys continued their taunting chant, "*Annie Fannie Farmer, Annie Fannie Farmer, Annie Fannie Farmer.*" I listened closer, feeling helpless. I could hear the sarcasm in their voices. All I could do was stare blankly at them and fight back the tears.

"You know you will just get hurt and go crying back home to your mommy. Go play with some dolls instead." Their taunting little chant continued, and they started to whisper to each other. I wasn't wanted here.

Don't let them see you cry, don't cry, be strong, crying is for girls, don't let them see you being a girl. I turned around, feeling embarrassed and humiliated. I walked back toward home with my head down and the tears started to stream down my face...

"See ya, Fannie, go have tea and cookies with your dollies."

My mind started to swirl…Fannie Farmer? What the hell does that mean? Fannie…Fannie…Fannie. The words slowly took on a meaning of their own.

Look at her fat Fannie. Annie has a fat Fannie. Look at that fat Fannie…fat Fannie…fat…fat…fat…I am fat, chubby, stocky, and not like the other girls. I look different. No wonder I don't fit in.

The seed that started my self-doubt. The words I took on as my own. Fat, *I am fat.* Those were the only words I heard. I had a fat Fannie, and I am fat. The early phrases "she's a chubby baby" and "she's built stocky and sturdy" came rushing back. Why else would they call me Annie Fannie Farmer? It *must* mean I am fat.

These words and phrases were planted deeply in my mind. I was not good enough, not right enough, not thin enough. I was different. All these thoughts began to flow together and attached themselves to more and more feelings. Soon these feelings became centered around my early adoption and to feelings of being unwanted and abandoned. More and more questions filled my brain.

Why didn't my birth mother want me? Why was I so different, why did I not look, act, or feel like other kids? I had short brown hair and looked like a boy. No ponytails or dresses for me like the other kids (because I hated them). Why didn't I fit in? My brain began to connect the dots. I felt outcast because I was chubby and fat and looked like a boy. It all was starting to make more and more sense. It's no wonder she didn't want me.

The only way I knew how to deal with all this was to start to shift my personality. I figured it was a good way to fit in, and the only way the other kids might like and accept me. I began watching the other kids. I observed, took notes, and became a nine-year-old detective, like Nancy Drew. How did the other girls act, look, talk, behave? I should be doing that. I came to the conclusion that I needed to shift, change, and copy how they acted. The imposter Anne was born. I was acting how I thought I should act, saying what I thought I should say, and began conforming to fit in. I became a master at hiding myself.

Every day, I would assess the people I was with, what they were like, and the situation. I then morphed into whoever I needed me to be so I would fit in.

Elementary school would be ending soon. I was glad. It was time for a new start. I had learned how to fit in here, so I knew I could do it again. Look out, junior high…

Watering the "Fat" Seed

I jumped in the car with my mom to head to the Liberty Tree Mall to get some new school clothes. I was excited to be heading to junior high. A new school, new people, new classes, and new experiences. A fresh start, all I wanted was to fit in and I knew getting some cool clothes would definitely help.

I wanted to wear what the popular kids were wearing. They wore cool jeans, and jackets, awesome flairs and striped sweaters. I was most looking forward to getting some great jeans. All the pants I had at home were polyester, uncomfortable and stupid. I hated them all.

As we walked into the big mall, my mom turned right, heading toward Sears on the corner. I whined and told her I wanted to try a different store this time. But she dismissed the thought and let me know Sears had the best selection for me and my body.

Hmmm. My body? What has my body got to do with any of this? I wear clothes to cover up my body. Why do I need to worry about that? All I want are some cool clothes with awesome colors, so I will fit in and the other kids will like me...

I sulked and dragged my feet into the girls' section. I ran toward the jeans and pulled out a pair. My mother cocked her head to the side, wrinkled her nose, and stated, "Jeans? No, no, no. We are here to get you a couple of nice dress pants. Ones that will fit you well and flatter your body." *I don't want dress pants! I don't care about flattering my body...I care about fitting in and dressing like everyone else.*

"I want jeans...that is what everyone else is wearing," I whined.

"If everyone else was jumping off a bridge, would you?" she questioned.

"Of course," I answered with a touch of sarcasm.

"Don't be wise with me. Here try these on, they look nice, and put those jeans away."

I took the stupid-looking pants made with the funny material into the dressing room. I started to put them on and couldn't get them over my thighs. "Mom," I yelled, "can you get a bigger size, these don't fit."

"There is no bigger size here," she yelled back. "Get dressed and we will head over to another department." *Good, these pants were stupid anyway,* I thought.

We walked out of the girls' department and turned toward the back of the store. We walked past the boys' section, past infants and the shoes. As we turned the corner, there it was: the big sign that read "Husky." Ugh, I knew exactly what that word meant: FAT. *Husky? What am I, a dog?* I thought sarcastically to myself. Within seconds, I was bombarded by the critical words of my Mini-Me. *No, you're not a dog, you're just a fat pig, that is what the boys call you…fat. It must be true; they must be right. You are fat! You can't even shop in a regular department; you have to go to the back of the store to find fat clothes for yourself.*

As we walked into the department; I was instantly deflated. I looked around and thought *NOTHING, I SEE NOTHING!* Mom made a beeline to a rack on the left and pulled out a pair of pants. She hustled over to another rack and pulled out a shirt, and a jacket.

"Here, try these on and come out and show me."

I walked over to get the clothes she was holding, pushing back the tears. The voice in my head kept repeating *don't cry, don't cry, don't cry.* I grabbed the clothes and with my head down trudged into the dressing room.

I pulled the first pair of pants up; they were tight on my thighs, but at least I could get them on. I threw on the shirt and jacket and went out to show my mom.

Her eyes lit up. "Oh…that all looks wonderful on you, turn around…those pants fit great. How do you like them?" she asked with hope in her voice.

I couldn't help but notice the light in her eyes. I didn't have the heart to tell her I was uncomfortable, that I hated them and just wanted to run out of the store and go home. So, before I knew it, I looked up at her and smiled. "Yes, Mom, I like them." It was a flat-out lie.

And even though it was not the first lie I had told my mom, it was the one that started the onslaught of years of lying, hiding, and deceiving.

Fertilization of Fat

A mere one week later, I walked into the cold, sterile doctor's office for my annual stupid "eleven year" visit.

"Good morning, Anne," the doctor stated and without hesitation continued, "Wow, have you gotten bigger since last year! Step right up here on the scale for me." I stepped on the scale. His eyes got big, he looked me up and down, headed to his desk, and jotted the number down.

He called my mom over to talk to her privately. "Pat," he stated solemnly, "she is way outside the normal growth chart right now. You must start watching what she eats. You don't want her to gain any more weight right now. She should just be eating her meals. No sweets or snacks. It must start now if you want to catch this in time." I see my mom nod.

I don't miss the doctor's words, actions, or looks. They just confirm to me what I already knew, what the boys in the neighborhood already knew, and what the husky section at Sears knew: I am fat. *Great, I am a fat, stupid tomboy. What a perfect way to go to junior high and fit right in,* I thought to myself. The doctor has just strengthened my belief that I am fat. It's official. Doctor approved. It's noted on the doctor's chart and seared into my brain.

Step Back:

1. What memories and experiences do you recall may have started the way you see yourself?

2. Are there identities of yourself you are still holding on to today?

3. Take some time to put the memories and identities together to come back to later. Build yourself a life experience time line.

My time line starts in 1963 and goes through today. On it, there is my adoption, kindergarten, first grade, sixth grade, all the way up to today. Every event I remember and feels important, I write on the time line where it belongs. You may also want to write some other events in there too. Things like, my grandmother went into the hospital, my sister broke her arm, my parents got divorced. As you create your time line, try to continue to be compassionate and kind to yourself. Think of yourself as a detective, travel through your life's experiences with curiosity.

CHAPTER 4

Gym Shorts

I STARED AT THE CLOCK AS I LEANED ON MY DESK, LOOKING RIGHT through it. Thank God it was almost time for gym class. All I could think about was the fact that in elementary school, it was the one place I fit in. I have been holding on to that thought all day. *Hurry up clock, this has been the longest friggin' day ever. At least gym class is a place where I can go and actually feel comfortable and fit in.*

It was my very first day at junior high and so far, it had proved to be the worst. I knew no one in any of my classes, feeling completely out of place and alone. I went from class to class with the hopes of seeing someone I knew. Yet all I saw were the pretty girls, with thin bodies, long hair, makeup, and skirts. I didn't see anyone familiar and no one who resembled the way I looked, that was for sure. And to make matters worse, of course, was that there was no one dressed like me. Stupid Sears "husky" pants and jacket. *I hate these pants, they are so friggin' tight!* I had been uncomfortable in them all day.

The bell finally rang, and I followed the group down the hall. A teacher told us to gather, and he began to lecture.

"We are heading into the high school for your PE class. Stay together as a group. No talking. You will head straight into your respective locker rooms to get fitted for your gym suits."

Gym WHAT? Are you kidding? Gym suits? What are those? Why can't we wear our clothes like we did last year? Shit, this means I have to change in front of these other girls. I need a trip to the nurse's room right now! I'm gonna throw up.

I stood in line with twenty-five other girls, my head down. They were conversing all around me. I felt invisible. We walked up one by one to a tall woman, standing in what looks like a closet. There were racks full of white and red pinstripe shirts and bright red shorts on one side and on the other side, bins and bins of balls and bats. Her glasses were propped on her head, and she had a whistle around her neck.

"What size?" she asked each girl who stepped up. Small, extra small, small, medium (ooohh…I look up). *I'll try that. A medium… that doesn't seem so bad.* Small, small, small… *Where the hell am I? SMALL world?*

I stepped to the window. "Medium," I said. She handed me a pair of red polyester shorts and a red and white pinstripe t-shirt. The shorts felt sticky and rough in my hand. My stomach began to tighten. *These feel just like the pants I have on.* I felt my eyes start to tear, so I hustled toward the back of the locker room. Small old gray lockers spread out to the right and left. I found a little corner in the back where no one else was. I took off my crappy tight pants and tried to put the crappy red shorts on. They don't fit; I can't get them over my thighs. *Shit, what am I going to do now?* My heart began to race, and I began to panic. I couldn't seem to get enough air. I felt paralyzed…*think, Anne, think… think!*

I ripped the shorts off and put my pants back on. I took off my jacket and shirt and tried the shirt on; it's tight too. It doesn't even fit my shoulders. *Great, just great.* My expectations of gym class have blown up right before me. How could gym class go from the highlight of my day at elementary school to a full-blown nightmare here? I peeled the shirt off my body, and I put my regular one back on. I folded up the gym shirt and shorts and took the long walk down the locker room to the small room in the front. As I did, all I saw was girls' bodies, girls' thin, small, petite bodies. I wanted to run far, far away. I didn't want to be here.

A girl looked up from tying her sneaker and wrinkled her nose at me. The shame shitstorm started swirling around in my head. *I hate my body, I hate myself, I hate this feeling.* A familiar wave of self-hatred washed over me.

The seeds of fat, stupid, clumsy, and messy were being watered and strengthened. The voice in my head started. *I can't look like this. I have to do something…I have to look like the other girls.* I have heard the other girls talk about going on diets and losing weight by not eating. *That's it,* I thought, *I will find a way to lose weight. I don't want to feel like this.*

I made my way up to the front of the locker room. The woman was still in the small room and looked up at me. "Why don't you have your gym suit on? Gym starts in two minutes," she snapped.

"Um…"

"Speak up, girl…what?"

"Um…I need a bigger size."

"OK, why didn't you just say so…what do you need?"

"A large?"

She turned and walked to the back of the room, looked around and then picked out some shorts and a shirt.

"Here, put these on, these should do. Now, hurry up."

I took them and turned back toward the aisle of the locker room. This time there were only a few straggling girls left, tying their sneakers with their heads down. I got to my space in the back, my eyes beginning to fill up once again. I ripped off my pants in anger and pulled up the shorts. *They are tight, tight, tight…fuck. I am not going back up there, I am not, I am not.* I finished getting dressed and put on the t-shirt, I stretch it…pull and tug at it to try to help it cover my butt. I pulled on the shorts with all my might, trying to stretch them out. I fell to a heap in the corner of the room with my head in my hands. I felt sick to my stomach. *Why am I so fat, why, why, why…?*

TWEEEEET…a whistle blew loudly in the locker room and pierced my ears. I lifted my head and hear the loud booming voice. "Everyone to the gym floor NOW…let's go, let's go…"

I wiped my eyes, threw all my clothes into a small locker, grabbed my sneakers, and ran. The next forty-five minutes were spent thinking of only one thing: *I am fat, the boys were right, the doctor was right, I am a fat ass, fat, fat, fat…*

That one singular thought spiraled my brain into a barrage of more thoughts. One thought after another. They came in so fast it was as if they had come from a playbook: *I have to lose weight, I will go to the library and get a book, there has to be a book on how to lose weight, I have to get thin and look like the other girls. Everyone is thin. People on TV are thin, people in magazines are thin…. What is wrong with me? Why am I this way? No one else has legs like me, no one else has a body like me, no wonder my mother didn't want me! I am fat…who would want a fat kid, never mind a fat baby. Look at that girl, look at her legs, I wish I looked like her.* I looked at my thighs pinched by the red shorts. *Look at that other girl, she has boobs already…* I looked at my chest…nothing. *All I see are my fat legs squished in these tight polyester red shorts, my flat chest. I hate gym, I hate school, I hate myself, I hate my body. Please God…help me. Help me lose weight and look like these other girls.*

The voices in my head were relentless, getting louder and louder, meaner and meaner. More judgment, more criticism, more shame. Captain Criticism had joined the voices in my head and became the boss of comparing me to all the other girls and criticizing me sharply.

A switch had flipped. Today was the day my relationship with food changed forever. Food was now the enemy. It had to be food that was making me fat. That was what the doctor told my mom. She had started to watch what I ate anyway. Just the other day she yelled at me when I tried to sneak a cookie from the cookie jar. "Anne Buffum Poirier! What are you doing in there!" she had yelled from across the house. How do parents do that? How do they know from another room what you are doing? *If I stop eating, I would make them happy and I would make the doctor happy. Less food starts now. And I will start to do sit-ups at night to make even more sure to get smaller. This will make everything OK. If my body is thinner, I will fit in. If I lose weight, I will be happy.*

I became absorbed in my head and trapped by my thoughts. In that moment I disconnected from what everyone else thought or said. I separated from my friends and what they cared about. I detached from the world completely, only to be consumed by my own thoughts of not being thin enough or good enough. I went into an obsessed place in my brain, full of voices that had things to say. These voices had strong opinions, harsh judgments and criticisms to share with me. I hated myself and my body.

The Voices Take Control

That night at dinner I took a small portion. I remember the meal and my plate, salmon and peas on saltines. I took three saltines and placed them neatly on my plate. I placed a single spoonful of the salmon and peas concoction on top of them. I ate with focus and complete disconnection from anything else going on at the table. As soon as I finished and excused myself from the table, I pushed back my chair and ran upstairs to start what was soon to be a punishing sit-up ritual. The voices told me what needed to be done. They gave me strict orders: eat less, exercise more, lose weight. *It is the only way you will survive in this world. It is the only way to fit in. Get thin and lose weight at all costs.*

From that day on, mealtime at the Poirier home became a counting, calculating math class. How many calories in this, how many calories in that? How many did I eat today, how many have I burned off so far?

Dinner with my family became a war zone.

"Eat your dinner," my dad would say. "Stop playing with your food," my mom would add. I moved the food around on my plate, trying to look like I was eating something, always hoping they weren't watching me.

My stomach would tighten up, my mind would go into a crazy whirlwind...counting calories. The voices in my head were relentless and endless. I would stop eating and just move the food around on my plate, my brain continuing to taunt me. Every once in a while I would take a bite. Just enough to appease them.

It was working. I could feel those red gym shorts were not cutting off my circulation as much anymore. But then, there was spaghetti night. My favorite. I loved spaghetti night. I loved the way I could twirl it on my fork, the way it tasted in my mouth. I was both excited and terrified. *I will just eat a little.* I served myself a small plate. Slowly, I started eating, one bite at a time, playing with my food in between each bite.

I could tell my parents were annoyed with me and this game I seemed to be playing. I thought they were judging me. I didn't want to disappoint them, so I began to eat a little faster. Before I knew it, my plate was empty. *AHHHH, how did that happen?* I didn't even remember eating it. The voices started in... *You are disgusting, you can't even control yourself.* I was mad at myself. One moment I was feeling in full control, righteous and perfect. In the next like a failure, weak, angry, and disappointed with myself.

Mini-Me started in... *You have no willpower, you are so stupid, so weak. Get up and leave the table now before you do even more damage. You have to burn that off, you fat pig. No food tomorrow for you... nothing. That might teach you.*

My thoughts continued to race. *I hate food, I love food, I can't stop thinking about food. How can I get out of eating all together?*

I left the table, calculating and counting in my head all the calories I wouldn't eat tomorrow. I headed upstairs, lay on my bedroom floor, and started my sit-ups...

Identity

I felt invisible and it was easy to blame my body for everything. It became the scapegoat for all my anger, sadness, loneliness, and frustration. It had to; it was the only thing I knew I could change. The lifelong journey began. Constantly seeking for a way to fit in. The only change that made sense to me was to change the way I looked.

I figured I was too fat for others to notice me. I couldn't wear cool clothes because they didn't fit me. *If I lost weight, people would see me, they would notice me, and my parents would be proud of me too.*

Step Back

1. How are the seeds you discovered in the last chapters linked to thoughts and behaviors you still have today?
   a. What beliefs have come from these thoughts and behaviors?

    b. Are these beliefs still instilled strongly in your mind?

    c. Are you willing to question these beliefs?

2. Are these beliefs linked to an identity you still hold on to?
    a. What was your earliest identity (smart, musical, distracted, anxious, stubborn, funny)?
    b. Does this identity serve you? And if so, how?

CHAPTER 5

Obsessed

DAY AFTER DAY...MEAL AFTER MEAL...SIT-UP AFTER SIT-UP. I counted and calculated, restricted, punished, judged, and criticized myself. Losing myself more and more every day. My obsession with food and my body became a full-blown eating disorder. Anorexia Nervosa erupted into my psyche. Thoughts of weight loss and calorie burning consumed and engulfed my mind and body. As I lost weight, I gained pride in myself. People said I looked good. The more weight I lost, the more attention I received. People actually noticed me. I was going to be thin, finally. I'd fit in and I'd be happy.

I was disappearing right before my parents' eyes. Obsessed with food, eating, exercise, and losing weight. I lied every day when they asked me what I had eaten for lunch. Each day, I would eat a few bites and the rest went into the garbage.

I was getting good at the deception. My parents began to worry.

I didn't care. I was too far invested in fitting in and being thin. I was finally in control.

Mirror, Mirror

In 1975, I am twelve years old and wearing only a pair of underwear. My mother is making me stand in front of a full-length mirror. I'm humiliated and mortified.

She is sitting on the bed with a very serious look on her face. My immediate thought was, *what the hell did I do to deserve this?*

She starts by asking me a point-blank question: "Look in the mirror and tell me what you see."

I roll my eyes and look into the mirror. "Yuck" is the first thing I see. Tears begin to well up. I am angry and disappointed in myself. I pinch the skin on my belly and state, "I see fat and frumpy, happy?" And that *is* exactly what I see. I see in the mirror staring back at me a body that is fat, ugly, and full of shame. Can't she see that? Everyone else does.

She senses my seriousness and realizes I actually believe what I am saying. She sees frail, fragile, and frighteningly thin. We are both looking at the same almost naked body yet seeing completely different things. We are thinking different thoughts and are experiencing opposing emotions. I think yuck and feel shame; she thinks sick and feels scared.

"Can I go now?" I say. I am feeling awkward and alone.

My mom nods. There is sadness in her eyes. She is terrified, tired, and feeling hopeless. She has been watching me disappear day by day in front of her eyes, unsure of what to do, or where to turn next.

All she knew was that I was not the Anne she remembered. Not the Anne she knew. It was like I had become overtaken by something outside of myself. She was right. I was detached, obsessed, and completely preoccupied with myself.

My mom was determined to help. She immersed herself in trying to find answers. There must be something she could do to help her disappearing girl. She turned to her friends and the library on a relentless search for answers. As I whittled away, she foraged forward. Then she found *Eating Disorders* by Hilde Bruch MD. As she read, she knew she found what she was looking for. This gave her a bit of control. She knew exactly what to do next.

The Enemy

I got in the station wagon, slamming the door and crossing my arms, and sulked in the passenger seat. Angry to be forced out of my daily rituals. At least my stomach was growling, so that made me happy. She started the car and off we went. There was both tension and anxiousness in the air. We drove in silence.

Through the town of Topsfield, we drove. We finally took a right onto Mansion Drive, a well-kept street with big, beautiful homes. I was in awe of the size of the homes and the bright green of the lawns. My mom turned into what seemed like the biggest and most beautiful of them all. It looked like a mansion...*Hmmm, must be why it is called Mansion Drive. Mom would hate to have to clean this place!* I thought.

I sat and stared at the large, dark, heavy double doors. "Go on," Mom said. "They're expecting you." I got out and scuffed my feet as I walked toward the big doors. "I will pick you up in an hour. It will all be OK," she stated with authority.

I walked my frail and frightened twelve-year-old body to the massive door and rang the gold bell. A nice old lady opened the door and gestured to me to come in. I followed her around the corner and down a hall. The home smelled like apples…my stomach growled. *I bet they did that on purpose*, I thought.

I followed the woman into a large room, through yet another large brown door. "Have a seat," she said. "The doctor will be right in." She turned and hustled out.

I stood frozen and looked around. The room was dark, and the walls were filled with rows and rows of books. *This guy must be really smart and really old to have all these books…this is going to be so booooring…* I thought.

As I looked around, I spied a big brown chair in the corner. I raced over and sat down. It seemed to swallow me up. I curled my legs underneath me, crossed my arms, and waited. I started to give myself a pep talk. *You got this; this will be easy. He is going to try to get you to eat. Just lie to him, like you do to your parents. You got this… no one can make you eat. This doctor is the enemy, don't let him ruin everything you have worked so hard for.*

I heard footsteps. My stomach jumped. *I have to throw up*, I thought. So much for the pep talk. The big brown door opened and in came this large man with a round belly and white beard. He kinda looked like Santa Claus. He was wearing a dark green sweater vest, brown loafers, and his glasses rested on the tip of his nose.

"You must be Anne," he said with a soft voice. I nodded, not moving. He stepped a little closer and bent down toward me, extended his hand, and said, "It is very nice to meet you."

I softened a bit, uncrossed my arms and unfolded my legs, and shook his hand.

Where the hell am I and what the heck is going on, what has my mother signed me up for now? I was feeling both scared and comfortable at the same time. Nothing I had ever felt before. *He actually seems to see me. He may even like me. Maybe he won't make me eat? Maybe he is different?*

He turned and moved his large swivel desk chair out from behind the large old desk. He sat down across from me and before I knew it, he was off talking. Rambling on, all about his day. He talked about the weather outside, how busy he had been, the book he was reading, and about what he had for lunch. I sat and listened curiously and cautiously…

Then he asked a simple question of me. "What did you have for lunch today, Anne?"

I drew a quick breath and started to panic. *Think, Anne, think. You do this all the time.* I took a deep breath, pretending it was Mom asking. My mind was swirling with doubt. *Don't tell him the truth, he doesn't deserve the truth… but you are hungry, you are always so hungry, maybe he can help?* My Mini-Me voice was confused, frightened, and yet ready to fight. I didn't know what to do or say. *No one knows about your rules and rituals, those are your secrets. Don't tell him anything, he could ruin everything you have worked so hard for. He is the enemy. He wants to make you fat.*

I took another deep breath, sat up tall, and began. "I had a peanut butter and fluff sandwich that my mom made me. I also had an apple and two fig newtons, oh, and my friend Leslie shared her chips with me, so I had some of those too."

I sat back in the big chair, feeling proud of myself…*this is going to be easy,* I thought.

He cocked his head to the side. "Wow, if I ate that for lunch, my belly might be even bigger than it is today!" He smiled as he laughed hard at his own joke.

It was no joke to me. He knew I was lying. Damn it, what am I going to do now?

"Want to tell me what you really had for lunch?"

"I am telling you the truth," I lie.

I held tight to my lunch story too, for many, many visits. I knew he was trying to fix me, and I wanted no part of this, he was my enemy.

Family Meeting

My brother was pissed, he was fifteen and had to go to some stupid shrink one Tuesday afternoon after school. Missing soccer practice too. He stared out the window as the whole family took a trip to Mansion Drive.

We all sat in seats in the big library office. I was sunken into my big brown chair, my brother across from me with his arms folded, and my parents on the couch in the middle of us.

My parents expressed their concern that it didn't appear I was getting "any better." Asking what they should be doing, how they could be of more help. I checked out. This wasn't about me at all. Until the middle of the meeting, when the doctor turned to my brother and asked, "What do you think of what is going on with Anne?"

He turned to the doctor and said, "I don't really care." And why should he? He was in high school now, figuring out his own way. Yet a flood of sadness came over me and I sank deeper into myself. *This is all so stupid, just leave me alone, all of you. My own obsession is grander than all of this and all of you.*

Eventually, the Mansion Drive therapist ended up sending me to the hospital because I broke a promise. From day one he told me if I dropped below a specific weight, he would admit me to the hospital. In the hospital they would be able to pump sugar into my body. I thought it was only a scare tactic, until it wasn't. Before I knew it, I went below the threatened low weight we had designated and off to the hospital I went. I was there for four weeks in the middle of summer. I don't remember much, my brain malnourished. I just know I lost more weight there before I started to gain it back. I hated all of this. I hated how much I was hurting my parents. I could see it when they visited. I was disappointing them more and more every day.

When I got out of the hospital, I continued to visit the man on Mansion Drive for over two years. In time, he slowly became my friend, my confidant, and the only person whom I could trust. Somehow, he began to open my eyes to seeing myself a little differently. He started to share with me how we need food to do the things we like to do. I was always cold, wasn't allowed to do anything, and had no energy. This was not making other kids like me; it was just isolating me even more.

This doctor slowly and patiently helped me find a way out of this dark, obsessed hole I had placed myself in with his kindness and compassion. With his nonjudgmental approach, his safety and honesty. I started to trust him with my rules and rituals. As we talked about them, he helped me see how they were connected to me never feeling good, always feeling freezing, always hurting. I started to eat again and as I did, I started to feel better.

Lost

From the first day of junior high, to the first day of sophomore year of high school, I don't remember much of anything. Everything that happened during that time are lost memories. I don't remember even going to school. All I remember are the fights at home around food, the never-ending calculations in my head, and the endless sit-ups in my room. I remember the hospital weigh-ins and a few of the many conversations in the big book room on Mansion Drive.

My three-year bout with Anorexia Nervosa was my way of fighting to be seen, to fit in. I was able to control the size of my body, and in doing so I found there were benefits. People paid attention to me and worried about me. They actually noticed me. Kids and grown-ups I didn't even know complimented me on how good I looked in the beginning. I was being seen. It felt so good and continued to strengthen my belief that thinner was somehow better. I became addicted to the feeling of being noticed. I liked the attention and wanted more and more of it.

From Anorexia to Addiction

Going into the summer after my freshman year, I was begging my parents to go to camp. It was the last year I would be able to attend before I would age out. The only way they would allow me to go was if I reached and sustained a particular weight and started to exhibit responsible eating behavior. This was during the same time I was opening up to the doc on Mansion Drive.

Easy peasy, I thought. And it was. The therapy had helped me realize what I needed to do so they wouldn't worry about me. And I wanted to be normal. I wanted to find friends, I wanted to go to camp and do things the other kids were doing. I wanted to be warm and I wanted to make my parents happy. My first step was to start eating more. I also figured I knew how to lose the weight if I needed to.

My weight began to stabilize and off to camp I went. I made a great friend there; her name was Ann too (without an E), and food seemed to drift into the background. I stayed active and began to once again have the energy to run and jump. When I came home ready to start school, I informed my dad that I wanted to try out for the soccer team. I had maintained my weight at camp, so my dad said yes, as long as I didn't start to backslide.

I switched obsessions, from the focus on being thin to being exceptional at soccer. If I became good enough, people would notice me for that. Another attention-seeking activity. Just being thin wasn't enough anymore. I was determined to become good enough to be noticed. Thin and a good soccer player, that will get my parents and my classmates to see me and appreciate me.

Soccer took over my brain as another way to gain approval. I replaced my dieting compulsiveness with soccer practice. I practiced for hours on end. Running, doing sit-ups, juggling, dribbling, kicking. All in the name of getting noticed: *Please see me. Please notice me, please tell me I am good, I am worthy, I am enough.*

My thoughts of being fat led me to dieting, restricting, and punishing behavior. I believed I was not worthy or good enough if I was not thin. Once thin became something my parents and doctor were tracking and keeping an eye on, I had to find something different to control. Soccer was it. As far as food was concerned, it was still part of the playing field.

Step Back:

    1. Take a look at your timeline from chapter 3. Are you

able to connect activities, hobbies, opinions, obsessions to some of your seeds and thoughts about yourself?

2. Are any of your seeds the foundation for what you don't like to do or try? (For example, I didn't care for drawing, art, painting, etc., due to the belief I was messy.)

CHAPTER 6

Rooting Beliefs

Yo-Yo Up

"Hey there, Anne, pants are getting a little tight," Dan announced as he walked by and patted my ass.

It was the summer after I graduated high school. I was seventeen and working at Wendy's. The manager, Dan, just called me fat, and he touched my butt...I freaked out. Not because he touched my butt, but because he just called me fat. Please, not that, anything but that.

I had been working there for about three months, and each day he had been paying more and more attention to me. Touching my lower back and getting close to me while teaching me something. I was flattered. A man was actually paying attention to me. Something I was certainly not used to. I actually liked it, until that day. That day he called me fat and touched my ass. Because now I knew he didn't like me; he was just making fun of me.

This was a catalyst for a combination of thoughts that came rushing into my head. *You know he is right. You have gained weight. You are disgusting. You have been eating way too much, your pants **are** tight. He finds you disgusting. Why can't you ever control yourself? You actually used to be skinny. No one would ever know it!* I put my head down and kept working as far away from him as possible, with these thoughts continuing to penetrate my brain.

All I could feel was how tight my pants were. A familiar feeling. It connected immediately to the thoughts and beliefs of the past. *How could you have let this happen? You can't be fat heading to college, you have to do something NOW.*

Calorie counts flooded back into my head; menus of what to eat and what not to eat came rushing in. *I can do this, I have done it before, how could I have let myself go like this? Wasn't it a mere couple years ago everyone was telling me to eat more? To actually try to gain weight?*

Before I knew it the Dexatrim commercial popped into my brain. *That's it, I will pick some up on the way home. That will help me control my stupid-ass self. I have the money to get it now and can keep it hidden in my room.*

I breathed in a sigh of relief. My plan was set. I figured out exactly what I would eat for breakfast, then eat whatever my mom served for lunch. This way they wouldn't notice anything unusual. As soon as I left for work at 3:30, I wouldn't eat anything else for the rest of the day, except drink Diet Coke.

This plan would work, and my parents would never know.

Like clockwork, I lied every night over the next five weeks about what I had for dinner to them. I had five weeks until the start of double sessions for soccer at Plymouth State College. I wasn't starting college fat. I had to lose weight. And fast. My focus was set, and I was ready.

My brain was once again consumed with calories in and calories out. My lying increased and continued.

I won't succumb to the "freshman fifteen," I thought with great certainty.

Food Freedom

College proved to be a testing ground, an open invitation, a food fest. One yummy meal at the dining hall led to peanut butter and fluff cracker binge parties in the dorm. Everyone was doing it. There were no parents there to shut down the fun. Everything tasted so good and I felt free from judging eyes on me. So, I ate. I ate to fit in, I ate in secret, I ate to calm down, I ate because it tasted so good, I ate because I was hungry. I knew I was gaining weight.

When I got home for Christmas vacation after my first semester at college, the scale was right where it had always been in the bathroom…calling my name to step on it. I succumbed and weighed myself that first morning home. I slowly looked down and promptly started to cry. I had done it again. The number on the scale and the way everyone looked at me told the whole story. I was fat once again. *One big fat failure.* Soon I projected my own feelings of shame and disappointment onto everyone else (my parents, friends, and relatives). I knew they were all talking about how much weight I had gained and were all disappointed in me.

Disappointment, shame, and judgment of myself were three emotions I was used to, and some of the most powerful emotions that contribute to my feelings of low self-esteem and self-worth.

I felt my parents' judgment of me. But that was nothing compared to the harsh judgment and criticism I was attacking myself with. As they watched what I ate, I began the next diet chapter of my life. Little did I know the yo-yo game had just begun.

Yo-Yo Down

Back to the drawing board. How was I going to lose the weight this time? Consumed again by that Mini-Me in my head. *Fat, stupid loser who has no control. You're a disappointment, you will never be thin enough, never good enough, you are such a failure at everything.*

Even though I thought my parents may have wanted me to lose weight, I also knew they would be worried about me. Worried about me falling back into an eating disorder, becoming obsessed and irrational, so I had to be sneaky this time. They couldn't know what I was up to. I had put them through enough already, I didn't want them to worry.

I put on my sweats and headed out for a run and I ran right down into town, to pick up a box of Ex-Lax. I had started hearing about it at the end of the semester from a friend. We began to commiserate around gaining weight. It was an instant connection. We actually became friends because we both wanted to lose weight. How sad is that friendship and connection due to hating our bodies. We validated each other on not being good enough in the bodies we had. We both believed being thin would magically fix everything. Thin was what we all were supposed to be.

The last week of school the two of us had spent hours standing in the supermarket magazine section. We searched and took notes on all the diets that appeared in front of us. We ended up buying three different magazines, all with great headlines on the front. "Lose ten pounds in a week," "Flatten your stomach with these four foods," "The amazing three-day diet."

It was comforting to have someone else feeling the same way I did. They too understood that being thin was all that mattered. She too realized if you are thin, you would be happy. People would notice you. You would be accepted.

The Christmas break Ex-Lax caper was a great big failure. By the end of Christmas vacation, all I was doing was spending a lot of time in the bathroom. And I was broke. This certainly was not worth the cramps and burning ass. I was glad I was heading back to school where I would be out of sight from my parents and their disappointment. I would find something that would work there.

The roller-coaster ride continued. I continued to seek and search for approval and acceptance. Up and down the scale I went. From one diet to the next. One day it was the grapefruit diet, the next the cabbage soup diet. Each and every one of these diets were followed by extraordinary binges. Binges on peanut butter and fluff crackers, ice cream, Doritos, and cookies. These binges were followed by sit-ups, workouts, and punishing runs outside and up and down the dorm stairs. For days after a binge, I was berated by an abusive, critical, demeaning, and destructive inner voice too. That Mini-Me, rearing her ugly head to make sure I knew how stupid, fat, and weak I was.

I was a prisoner of my own thoughts and behaviors. Eat, not eat, pound my body into the ground. Up the scale, down the scale, and up the scale again. It haunted me until it was time to head back to school and pre-season soccer my sophomore year.

The Weigh-in to Worthiness

I woke up that first morning of preseason horrified. We all had to get "weighed in." As soon as I opened my eyes, I felt an instantaneous flood of fear, regret, guilt, and criticism. What would the almighty judge of the scale say today about my worth? Our skinny college soccer coach would stand judge and jury as we all stepped on the scale. (She was tiny, tough, and pushed us all to be our best, expecting us to leave it all on the field each and every day.) The weigh-in was her way of seeing if we had "done the work" that summer. I could taste the bile in my mouth.

I waited in line to face her, wanting to just run away. I was feeling suffocated. The lump in my throat was getting bigger and bigger and I was feeling smaller and smaller. More and more ashamed of myself.

I started justifying my summer in my head. I had worked out, so I knew I was in shape. I knew I could run the distance she asked of us last year. *I have to be OK. She will be proud of me for putting in the work,* I continued to tell myself to ease my anxiety.

I was next, shit, everyone was doing so well. *Please god, wherever you are, let me have lost weight, let her be proud of me...she has to be proud of me.* I stepped on the scale; she looked at the number then turned and looked me up and down. She paused and stared, her eyes piercing into my head and heart.

"What did you do all summer Anne, **EAT?**"

That was all she said and all she had to say to start me swirling. I was mortified. *I am such a fuckin' loser. I probably won't even make the team due to this. My dad is going to be so mad and disappointed in me.*

I stepped off that piece of metal without a word and walked out of the locker room.

I started visualizing the dining hall food. Before I knew it, I was counting up all the calories I would not be eating there. My mind on hyperdrive, I quickly concocted the perfect "diet" I would eat every day for the rest of the season. *I will show her...*

The days went by, one by one, with no joy, no emotion. I was running on empty in more ways than one. My love for soccer was gone, lost with each meal I denied myself. Where there once was light there was darkness. Where there once was laughter there was disappointment.

The spiral continued...the dieting, the laxatives, the extra runs. It felt like I was right back in junior high, withering away and trying to lose weight, all in the name of worthiness. It was all I knew. I knew how to deprive myself and beat myself up. At least I was good at that.

The seeds of belief that were planted so many years ago had formed roots in my brain. They had grown deeper and deeper year after year. Familiar thoughts continued to infiltrate my brain.

What am I going to eat next? How many calories are in that? How many calories have I eaten? How many calories have I burned off? How much more exercise do I have to do?

I compared what I ate with my thin teammates, compared my thighs to theirs. Compared my kicks, my stamina, my speed. Never good enough, thin enough, strong enough, fast enough.

It was a consistent, repetitive process of beating myself up over. I would call myself names to try to motivate me. *You're so stupid (fat, lazy), such a loser, such a failure, etc. It is no wonder you don't fit in. You will never fit in.*

I lived my college years in worry, hatred, and judgment, constantly in the future or the past. How can anyone remember any details of their life if they are constantly beating themselves up? No wonder college is such a blur.

The calculation of minutes exercised and calories burned was a never-ending lie. It was all my life revolved around. What was portrayed on the fake outside was strength, stamina, determination, and drive. On the outside, I was complimented on being dedicated, and strong willed. Yet on the inside it was all just an obsessive addiction: Eat less, move more. My body could only sustain short bouts of this though. After every period of restriction and, or bout of compulsive exercise, I would find myself in the middle of a midnight binge, quickly undoing any "work" I had done that day.

Something was not working. This pursuit of trying to have the perfect body was taking up every moment of every day.

Step Back

1. List your identities (mother, daughter, people pleaser, clumsy, procrastinator, etc.).

2. Where have they come from?

3. Which ones support how you think about yourself? And which ones sabotage or hinder you?

CHAPTER 7:

The Neighborhood

THE PERSPECTIVES I HAD OF MYSELF WERE THE RESULT OF THE SEEDS that were planted in my brain as a child. They led me to form a series of thoughts, behaviors, and beliefs. They have all come together and been interpreted by me to form my identity.

I interpreted what I saw and heard around me, what I experienced and the emotions I felt. I placed great value in what those around me thought. I knew there had to be truth in their words and actions. The more important the person, the more value I placed on what they thought.

The thoughts and beliefs I placed in my brain continued to search for ways to be proven to myself. My brain was primed and ready to find proof from whatever was around me. So, when the doctor told my mom, "You need to watch what she eats," I knew I needed to lose weight more than anything in the world. My young brain thought that if I lost weight, everything would be

OK. I would be accepted, noticed, seen, and liked by my teachers, friends, and parents.

I had formed a particular perspective of food, eating, my body, and myself. It was from these perspectives I made decisions. I made decisions I thought I "should" make in order to "make sure" I was accepted and approved of.

My role was to make sure I was thin enough, smart enough, pretty enough, and talented enough. If I was, then others couldn't make fun of me and my parents would be proud of me. I wanted to make my parents proud. It was them after all who'd decided to bring me home and raise me. I wanted to make sure I proved to my adopted parents it had been worth it. Because of my own interpretation of the experiences around me, I felt unworthy of their love. I needed them to know I was worth it.

The very first diet became an important experience rooted in my brain. I was convinced losing weight and being thin was what was expected of me. If I were thin, everything would fall into place. I would fit in at school, my parents would love me, and others would accept and approve of me too.

Weight and food were the only things I cared about. All in the name of this need to be liked, appreciated, noticed, and seen. It was the one thing that had tied my life together up to this point. I continued to seek something outside of myself to prove my worth and to show myself I matter. The answer was always my weight or weight loss. If I were thin, people would see me. If I were thin, I would be enough. If I were thin, I would be happy.

This conscious drive to be thin continued as an endless need to be seen. The belief and perspective smothered me. It is no wonder the belief grew stronger. The belief became my identity. It was just who I was. It was my story.

I became who I thought others wanted me to be. I went from obsessed about food and calories to being obsessed with being noticed on the soccer field. I became a soccer player. It felt natural, like I had reclaimed my "jock-tomboy" status and had formed a new identity for myself. In college I was known as a "soccer player." Before long, being a soccer player wasn't enough. I was constantly scared of messing up. College was different from high school. More pressure to be perfect. Pressure not to screw up. The team was full of great soccer players who never seemed to make the mistakes I did. I was hard on myself. With every mistake, I would get down on myself and beat myself up. Days later, I would still be thinking about a bad play I made. Angry, disappointed, and upset with myself. No matter how good I became, I never seemed to be good enough. I don't even really think I knew what "good enough" even looked like.

The Mini-Me's

My past experiences and thoughts birthed a group of Mini-Me's in my head. They soon formed a neighborhood there. It all started with one voice that told me I was clumsy, Clumsy Carla. She then made friends. I thought for sure all these "Mini-Me voices" were me. These thoughts were true. They defined who I was. It is time to introduce you to some of them...

1. ***You're a failure Phyllis***. *I'm such a failure, I am a loser, I am so pathetic, I can't do anything right.* She comes out whenever I do something wrong, screw up, or when I make a poor decision. She pops up whenever I am feeling overwhelmed, am having a hard time making a decision and can't seem to figure things out. "You're a failure Phyllis" would show up in times of indecisiveness. She shows up today when I do something "wrong." This has a similar voice to my college soccer coach and my mom and dad.

2. ***You're a fat pig Paula.*** *I am disgusting.* This is the voice of a little girl. This voice comes from nicknames, gym class, shopping for clothes, and doctor visits. She would show up most of my adult life, whenever I saw small, "thin," and fit women. Or when I look in the mirror and see cellulite on my legs, notice my protruding belly, or when my clothes are tight. When I feel uncomfortable with others or see other people look me up and down. Or even when I see people I haven't seen in a long time. This voice sounds a lot like me. The words and phrases that I made up due to the way people looked at me and by the way I looked at me in the mirror. She's disgusted with me. She sounds a lot like my pediatrician's disappointment and the massiveness of what society has deemed and portrays as "right."

3. ***Stupid Sally.*** Stupid Sally started with Clumsy Carla and Messy Mel from kindergarten. I was like a "bull
in a china shop." Her voice came from always breaking
things and hurting myself. When this happens, I link it
to being stupid for getting hurt, or not paying attention.
She would also show up when I didn't understand what
people were talking about or couldn't figure something
out (that I think I should be able to). She shows up today
whenever I break something, hurt myself, or don't pay
attention. She also speaks up when I don't know what to
say or do. This voice sounds like my first-grade teacher.

4. ***Captain Criticism.*** She comes from never feeling
thin enough, good enough, smart enough. From never fitting in because I said something inappropriate or
looked out of place. She shows up today when I start
to compare myself with other people. Whenever I start
to think I should "look like that" or "do it that way."
Other thoughts like "I will never be thin enough, smart
enough, fit enough, successful enough…" This voice
has the sarcasm of my ex-husband.

My own thought neighborhood came to live right inside my
brain. They have been sleeping in my bed, eating in my kitchen,
and hiding in my closet. They should be living down the street or
across the country. I recruited all these voices into my head, and
they have helped me move through my life. They have been my

companions. I have gotten very comfortable inside this neighborhood. The words and phrases they repeat are familiar. It is what I have always known. If I were to think differently, I would not be as comfortable. (More on this in a later chapter.)

These Mini-Me's brought all their bags that were fully loaded with ammunition. They know exactly what to say and continue to learn more and more ways to keep themselves heard by me every year. That has been their job, to get their voices heard.

They kind of remind me of a sports team. Sometimes they work together by passing the ball back and forth, feeding off each other. Other times they compete against each other, trying to make sure their voice is the loudest.

All these voices have contributed to strengthening my beliefs. They have developed, created, and strengthened the way I think about myself. These voices have solidified my perspectives around my weight, body, food, eating, exercise, and self-worth. My identity.

I have lived my life listening to these voices and trusting this neighborhood. Because of this, I have held myself prisoner to my own perspective.

I continued to sit inside this prison, within a home I have created with these voices. I have taken in and believed all their words, thoughts, and beliefs…and yet, the door is wide open for me to leave…

Comfort

I thought these thoughts and voices were my friends. They have kept me company when I have felt all alone. They know me, understand me, and are of comfort to me. They prove to me I am right. The comfort comes because they protect me from the words and hurt of others. If I can degrade myself, then others can't hurt me. No matter what anyone else can say, I get to say, "Yup, you're right, I already know that." *You're going to have to try harder than that to hurt me.* I have told myself much worse. My voices are my protection from being hurt by others.

So why wouldn't I continue to listen and engage with them? Especially in times when I am feeling stressed, threatened, exposed, or in danger. They come right alongside me to help navigate my stress. It is the natural "fight, flight, freeze" response that comes up due to my own self-protection system.

Every time I felt any undesirable feeling or emotion, there was an automatic and deep desire to move away from it. I had rooted in my belief system certain thoughts and feelings were wrong. I interpreted them as threatening. "Don't be angry because you lost the game, that is just a part of playing." "Don't be sad because your brother doesn't want you to go, he is older than you." "You can't be mad at Grandma, she is doing the best she can, you have to love her." Anger, sadness, frustration, jealousy are all emotions I believed to be wrong. Emotions I was not supposed to feel. And I certainly should not be showing them to others! They were unwanted and uncomfortable. So, in order to feel safe and more comfortable, I turned to my inner neighborhood and listened to what they had to say. *Being mad at that is stupid. You shouldn't feel like that. If you get mad, they will hate you. Why are you so sensitive? He has every right to do that and you don't, because you don't know how to act. If you get mad at her, she won't love you anymore.*

What they said was familiar. I would call myself names, beat myself up, and then turn around and run to something to numb it all out. All I wanted was to not feel the uncomfortable feelings and stop the incessant chatter. In order to do that, I checked out. Numbing out was my way of disconnecting. My "vices" included searching for a new diet, going for a run, pouring a drink, or binging on whatever was available.

It is no wonder I would begin with the old comfortable, consistent, and familiar thoughts of beating myself up and quickly turn toward something else that would provide me comfort and control, like food, restriction, alcohol, and exercise...

The seeds of unworthiness and "not enough-ness" were planted early and proved over and over again. It was because of this garden of belief I had planted that I was always trying to fit into a size I was not...no matter what size I was! I could never be small enough and my mind was consumed with food, eating, weight, and exercise. My beliefs about myself continue to be strengthened by the experiences, thoughts, and behaviors rooted in my head.

Step Back

    1. Who lives in your neighborhood?

        a. Can you recognize the voice? Who might it be? (Sometimes I hear an old coach, my brother, or my parents in my head.)

        b. Where might this voice come from (what seed)?

PART II
GROWING ROOTS

CHAPTER 8

Pumpkin

I STUDIED EXERCISE SCIENCE IN COLLEGE. I FIGURED IF I HAD A JOB in fitness, it would make me stay thin and fit. It was a way to keep my weight and myself in control. Fresh out of college I accepted a job at Cedardale Athletic Club for $5.00 an hour. No way I could afford an apartment of my own, so I lived at home for a while.

I was back in the home that had that same scale located in the same exact spot in the upstairs bathroom. Right across from the toilet, where it had always been. Both of my parents weighed in every day. They were conscious of their weight. Being trim was a sign of good health. That stupid scale called to me every day to check in. "Come on, Anne…see how worthy you are today!" it would scream. I continued to give in, day after day. It was my duty. I had to make sure I was a respectable weight. I had to look the part, you know, being a fitness professional and all.

That scale became the master of my present and the director of my life. If the number was one I liked, everything was OK, I was OK. If the number was not, I was not, I didn't deserve to be OK. I wasn't allowed to be happy. How could I be happy if I was not thin and fit? Was that even possible?

It didn't seem like it. Everywhere I turned I would see ads and commercials about how to lose weight. It started with the Tab ads I saw on TV at ten. Then on to the multitude of magazines with headings you couldn't help but see standing in line at the grocery store or drugstore.

I could go to the library and find shelves full of diet books, all promising a better future. It's no wonder I succumbed to society's "Thin Ideal" standards. It was all around me and all I knew. Thinner had to be better. Thinner had to make you worthy. Thinner was the answer.

The problem was, it didn't matter what size I was, I was feeling empty. Was this all there was? The job was OK, but not very fulfilling. I knew what I was doing and all, but I still didn't feel like I fit in with the other members of the fitness staff. Something was still missing. Where was the happiness I was supposed to be feeling? Why wasn't I feeling better?

So I started to search for something to help me feel better. Before I knew it, I was back searching for something to eat. Food always seemed to do the trick. It gave me instantaneous, albeit fleeting, relief. When I was eating something yummy, a wave of peace, relief, and satisfaction washed over me. For the immediate moment, I was free. It was *this* feeling I was continuing to search for. The problem was, as soon as it washed over me, I was knocked over by a second wave of shame, guilt, criticism, and judgment. Mini-Me and friends joined the party.

They were loud and obnoxious. Hard to ignore. With them always in my head, I began to feel pressured to do something about it. Maybe they were right? I was feeling lonely, stressed, and judged once again by the way I looked and felt in my body.

I headed back to the grocery store checkout to scope out the side of the lane where the magazine rack was located, full of that promising future. On the other side, there were rows and rows of candy bars.

Buy this magazine and start this diet. But before you do, why not have a "last supper" of a bunch of candy bars. They will be the last ones you will ever eat. Might as well enjoy them!

There was a headline for some magical three-day diet I heard about in a women's magazine. Lose up to ten pounds in three days. Hard-boiled eggs, hot dogs, grapefruit, toast. Anyone else remember that one? It looked perfect. I can do that! I couldn't wait to step on the scale after those three days to see that magic number on the scale.

I woke up on the morning of day four, hungry and thankful it was over, looking forward to something tasty for breakfast. But before I could allow myself to do that, I stepped on the scale. I looked down and felt the tension rise in my chest. *Don't you know how good I have been? Don't you know that I have done everything right over the last three days? They said I would lose ten pounds... fuckin' scale...* I stepped off it and gave it a swift kick. "You suck",

I yelled to the piece of metal on the floor and turned to the mirror to repeat the phrase "You suck" to the image staring back at me.

I can't believe how stupid you are. How fat you are. You do know that no one will ever like you. You are a piece of shit. Can't even follow a friggin' diet and lose weight right. You can't do anything right. You might as well just curl up in the corner. No one cares about you. Your mother didn't even care about you. She took one look at you when you came out and said, UGH…give her away, I don't want an ugly, fat kid. No wonder you can't control yourself. You are a loser, have been and always will be. Let's go get a fucking ice cream…that will show you…

My Mini-Me was even meaner and more degrading than ever. The leader of my thoughts and beliefs. Her assistant was the scale. Together they directed my choices and decisions.

Living at home, the scale and Mini-Me were drowning me. I knew I had to get out on my own. That would be the answer. It would ease up the pressure and make me happy. If I could live by myself and not have to answer to anyone or have anyone watch what I eat, I would be OK.

So, I went on a search for a new job with better pay.

Firefighters Needed

The ad in the paper almost jumped out at me. *Hmmm. Firefighter. That seems cool. People will think that is impressive. I haven't really heard of many female firefighters. This could be a job where I could make a difference and people would notice me.* I filled out the application that afternoon.

After the six-month series of interviews, written and physical tests were complete, I was hired as the first female firefighter in Salem, New Hampshire, along with three other guys.

I did everything in my power to fit in. To be good at the job. To earn respect. I worked hard and socialized outside of the job hard, trying to connect, be seen and gain acceptance. I would spend nights off at the Elks, drinking and playing darts. Talking like a guy, making sarcastic jokes, laughing at their conversations. I studied hard at learning the job. Street routes, fire safety, suiting up, flow pressure, dressing a hydrant. One night I snuck into the unisex bathroom (before they were the norm) and put up a poster of Jean-Claude Van Damme, just to see if I could get a reaction. I ate subs, pizza, and Chinese for dinners, lifted weights to stay strong, and kept my hair short to stay in regulation. It was working too; they all seemed to accept me. And I especially loved the way a person's face lit up when I told them what I did. I was actually feeling good about myself.

Pumpkin

I came into the firehouse kitchen after fighting a dumpster fire with a sweaty face and grabbed a Diet Coke out of the fridge. The smug cop who sat at the table with his coffee looked up and said, "Hey, it's Pumpkin. You know," he paused, "you look just like a pumpkin when you get out of the fire truck in your gear." He turned and smiled at the guys around the table. "You know, all round and yellow." I stared at him, wondering if he could sense my anger. I turned and walked away, trying to fight the tears. I had been in the fire department for over a year now. All I could think was, *"Am I really that fat again?"*

The words continued to swirl around in my head. Pumpkin, fat, round. Geeez, not again. I hadn't stepped on a scale all year. Weight for the first time in I could remember was not something I was focusing on. I was just focusing on being strong enough and capable enough to do the job at hand. I was just trying to fit in.

Old thoughts and beliefs started to fill my mind. *I'm sure I have gained weight. My pants do feel tight. I should find out. I have to find out, I can't be a fat firefighter. That is not acceptable!* The fat seed is still rooted deep inside. Pumpkin = Fat.

Early the next day I took a trip across the street to the health center to get a checkup. I knew they would have to weigh me, so I could find out how much damage I had done. So, per routine, I stepped on the scale. There it was. A number I had never seen before staring me in the face. I couldn't move. I stood there staring. Mini-Me voices swiftly, strongly, steadily started in. My chest became heavy, my stomach started to knot up, the tears started to form. *How the hell did this happen? How the hell have I gained so much weight? …I'll tell you how, Anne, by eating burgers, Chinese food, and pizza. By eating whatever else the "guys wanted." You did this to yourself by trying to fit in. You can't eat like the guys; you should have known that. You are disgusting, you fat slob…no wonder that cop called you Pumpkin, you deserve it. You have to go on a diet NOW and lose this weight!*

Just like that I spiraled back into dieting obsession, disordered eating patterns, and overexercise. Needless to say, it didn't take me long to find out what might be the next answer. The problem was, there were so many choices now! Weight Watchers, Atkins, Jenny Craig, Deal a Meal. I checked the phone book and picked my savior. The winner this time? Jenny. Jenny Craig to the rescue. I started my new diet plan. I also got myself back to the gym. It called to me every morning and every night. Pumpkin, my ass...I wouldn't let some smug, arrogant cop call me fat ever again.

An all-too-familiar story: if I lose weight, everything will be OK. A decision I made, due to how someone else perceived me. They must be right, and the only answer was to lose weight. If I did, I would be OK. I would be seen, appreciated, and liked. Maybe even by men.

Fitting In

Always trying to impress others and be someone everyone liked was my MO. Agreeing with opinions I didn't even have an opinion on. Agreeing with thoughts that actually made me angry. Allowing myself to be small and making sure everyone else knew what was best for me. This way of thinking was the way I lived. It was the story I told myself. I knew I wasn't good enough, smart enough, or thin enough to think I knew any better. These beliefs about myself, just rooted deeper and deeper into my brain.

I had been living my life seeking outside of myself for validation. If it didn't come, I would blame my body weight, size, and shape. If it was OK, I was OK. I was in a constant state of playing the "When I... then I ..." game. When I weigh this, when I look like that, or when people like me, *then* I will be happy. *Then* I will like myself. *Then* everything will be OK.

I spent hours, days, and weeks worrying about what someone was going to think about how I looked, what I did, or something I said.

The beliefs I had about myself continued to grow stronger and deeper. This search to be seen, accepted, and validated by others and feeling unseen is not an uncommon phenomenon. I am not the only one who tried something out of the ordinary to do this. Many women I know have isolated, broken the law, or turned to drugs or alcohol. Many have lost weight, gained weight, bullied or blamed others, or hurt themselves or others. All in the name of trying to find a way to feel better in the short term. All because the feeling of being rejected and not good enough hurt too much.

I thought being on the fire department would bring me the status and acceptance I was looking for. It was a "When I...." decision that left me with a "then I...." still feeling less than instead of feeling proud. Mini-Me was having the time of her life.

Step Back

1. What experiences have you had that have triggered you into old thoughts and behaviors?

2. How do you handle feeling uncomfortable?
   a. Do you turn to something to make you feel better?

CHAPTER 9

Running

HIS DEEP BLUE EYES WERE ON ME AND I KNEW IT. THEY PENETRATED me all night. It felt exciting and terrifying at the same time. The off-duty firefighters were all out for their normal Thursday night outing. I was the only female in the bunch. I had been in the fire department for a little over a year when things started to change with this man.

I am not sure I remember a man looking at me like that ever before. I was almost thirty and had only one boyfriend in college for about six months, before I broke it off because I freaked out. This might be my last chance.

We started to talk more and more. I felt a growing internal nervousness and excitement. Soon, we began to date in secret, not wanting the other firefighters to know about us. Not only was being in a relationship exciting, but it was also exhilarating to be keeping it a secret. It gave me a rush of adrenaline. He was blond, a little taller than me, strong and solid. He was opinionated, smart, and sarcastic and didn't care what anyone else thought about him. I think that is what drew me to him. I didn't want to be controlled by what other people thought about me either. Maybe being with him would help me feel like that too. We had interesting conversations and went out drinking together. I morphed into the woman I knew he would fall in love with.

He drank too much; so did I. As our relationship developed, we moved in together and slowly shared it with others. The longer we were together, the later and later he would come home from his shifts. So, because I had experienced firsthand the complaining and teasing the men did about their wives and girlfriends at the firehouse kitchen table, I had vowed to never do that. I promised myself I would never be the "nagging girlfriend." I would understand. So that's what I did. I just let it go. Never once telling him it bothered me, or that I wish he had called to let me know he was going to be late. We were both still independent firefighters, right?

After over three years of dating, I decided to leave the fire department and took a job at a gym so we could be together. We got engaged and planned to elope two weeks later.

Getting married would make me and my parents happy and would for sure make me feel grown-up. One night, a week before we were planning to elope, I came home late from working at the gym. The women I worked with threw me a last-minute bachelorette party. It was two in the morning and he was steaming. I had called to let him know I was going out, but he wasn't expecting me to be that late. He angrily questioned me about where I was, how dare I stay out so late, and stormed out of the house. I was so angry. The voice in my head kept thinking, *it is OK for you to come home at two but not for me? I don't think so.* I vividly remember standing on our deck that night, taking the engagement ring off my finger and throwing it toward him as he drove away. We were married a week later.

During the first year of our marriage, I was busy working at a gym, teaching classes and working the front desk. I loved my boss and the members there. It felt as though I was back in my happy place. My husband was still in the fire department, going out with the guys and taking extra shifts for the extra money because we needed it. We didn't see much of each other, and when we did, we connected quickly through drinking.

The Choice Not to Run

It was almost eight p.m. when I pulled around the corner and saw the gray pickup in the driveway. My heart sank. Dammit. He is home, I don't even get five minutes to myself...I thought for sure he would still be out.

I could feel the lump in my throat begin to form; it seemed to get bigger by the second. My stomach tightened up. *Why do I always seem to be feeling like this?*

I had been teaching classes at the gym and the happiness and joy from the energy there had quickly worn off. I so wanted to bask in that temporary happiness for just a little longer. My classes always perked me up. I parked the car and sat there staring at the perfect little square house. I fell in love with it at first sight, so happy to be taking such a grown-up step to buy it and move in with him. So optimistic, so naïve.

I opened the car door and got out. My heart was still pounding. I secretly hoped he would be asleep. I trudged to the front door, easing it open. The stale stench of beer hit my face. It never gets familiar. The loud snore echoed from the bedroom. I sighed with relief. A surge of thought came washing over my brain and penetrated my heart. *Go, now. Pack your bags and run away…run far, far away.*

Another voice chimed in: *What good would that do? It wouldn't matter.* Yet another voice said, *"what would your parents think?"* A fourth voice said, *"They would think you were weak, stupid and irresponsible."* To which a fifth voice affirmed *"You would disappoint them yet again."* I knew the voices were right. Everyone, including my parents would think that I didn't try hard enough, gave up and failed.

I can hear it now, *can't even keep yourself married for a year.*

I slipped off my shoes and tiptoed into the bedroom. In a trancelike state, I stripped off my clothes and threw on my baggy sweatpants and tee shirt. I climbed into bed and closed my eyes, hoping not to wake him.

Before drifting off to sleep, I sighed to myself and thought of the phrase my mother used to say: "You've made your bed, now you have to sleep in it." How ironic.

Stupid Sally was wide awake, making sure I knew running away was the dumbest idea I had ever had. Seeds had taken root;

beliefs had grown strong. I was living in the circumstances of my own choices and beliefs.

Children

The choice to get married came from a feeling of true worthiness this man gave me. I felt special. He seemed to really like me. That was more than I had ever imagined. I so wanted and needed to feel wanted and loved. I was determined to make this marriage work.

Having a child together would change things. It would help fill the hole that continued to be empty within me. I wanted to be a mom. To care for someone else and have someone need me. As luck would have it, after only six months of trying, I became pregnant.

Pregnancy was like a breath of fresh air. I felt free. I wasn't worried about calories, I wasn't worried about my body, I didn't care what other people thought. I was creating another human in my body and I loved every minute of it. My body and I finally had purpose. I craved peas and mashed potatoes, ate ice cream and cookies, and gave up wine without a second thought. It was nine months of bliss. Our first daughter entered the world after eighteen hours of labor, exactly on her due date and two days after my thirtieth birthday.

Within a mere few hours of wonder and joy, the thought of getting back into shape infiltrated the bliss. You see, they don't tell you that after you give birth to a baby, your stomach still looks like you are six months pregnant. I was horrified. *I couldn't go back to work looking like this.* I had to prove to everyone that I was hard core and disciplined. Once again, I was searching for external validation.

I wanted to prove to people I could get back into shape at record speed. I started working out at home three days after giving birth.

The You're a fat pig Paula Mini-Me voice was a constant companion. *"You're disgusting, how could you have let yourself eat like that for the last nine months! You know what you have to do,"* she would say.

The voice was relentless, constant, and mean. I couldn't seem to shut it up. So, between feeding the baby and pumping breast milk, I was doing sit-ups on the floor. I was pacing the house holding her, rocking her, and dancing with her. Moving my body any way I could, all to try to burn calories and take off the baby weight.

I was back teaching aerobics exactly four weeks later with three bras on, and a pair of Depends under my spandex. This was my new normal.

Before long, I knew I wanted this beautiful, perfect baby to have a sibling. Someone to hang out with, play with, love.

One More Time

As soon as I had this thought, it seemed, I was pregnant again. *And I could breathe again!* The set of handcuffs I had placed on myself had permission to be unlocked and removed. I could let my guard down and relax. I had been beating myself up to prove that I was a dedicated and fit "fitness professional." Prove that I could whip myself back into shape quickly after giving birth, like the movie stars did.

See me, notice me…

Pregnancy once again gave me "permission" to take a break.

Both a mental and physical break. Taking a break had never been part of my vocabulary before my first pregnancy. I had grown up pushing, doing, going, working, thinking, making choices, being productive. It took being pregnant for my mind to pause and give me the OK to relax. *"You deserve to take a break, because you are making another human being. You are supposed to take it easy and slow down!"* I was searching for moments of being allowed to rest.

This pregnancy was different though, because it came with another baby in tow. I was working, pregnant, and taking care of a baby who was becoming a toddler. I was in full demand and running on all cylinders, needed by all.

Baby two came early and my need doubled. These little people relied on me. They needed me and I needed them.

A couple of days after the birth of our second daughter, I looked down at my stomach. *Damn, I forgot what I was left with after birth.* A saggy fat stomach and out-of-shape body that squirted out pee every time I coughed, sneezed, or laughed. Ugh, back at it I went.

With two kids in tow this time when I went back to the gym to work. The girls became fast friends with the gym day care. They had to, because I dove right back into my multiple-class-a-week schedule. This was who I was, this was what I did.

My husband was working, doing overtime shifts, hanging out with the guys and doing his thing. He was the financial footing of our home. My "aerobics" money was just supplemental. The girls were with me most of the time. Unfortunately for them, I tended to be distracted, dragging them to the gym daily and completely overconcerned with my weight and appearance. How I appeared to others and what others thought of me was what I cared about.

It occupied my mind from the moment I woke up and chose my clothes for the day to the calculations of calories I did at the end of the night. Because of this, I wasn't very present at home. I was impatient, grumpy, moody, and short-tempered to both my girls and to my husband. Continuously worried about what everyone else was thinking. *Putting the opinions of others ahead of my own or my family's.*

I would drag them to the gym for an extra workout, bribing them with a trip to McDonald's afterward. I would take them to the mall shopping, just to get out of the house, let them eat whatever they wanted for dinner, because their dad was working. I remember getting angry with one of my daughters because she would always get up out of bed as soon as she heard me mulling around in the mornings. I just wanted to have a couple minutes by myself with my cup of coffee. The years went by and I missed many moments with them. It was much like junior high. I seemed to be somewhere else. Moving through the motions and disconnected.

I also felt like a single parent much of the time. Alone and lonely. I began wanting to take some time for myself, which only led to feelings of guilt and shame. So I didn't. What kind of mother wants to take time away from her kids? A horrible one, that's who.

Not only was I feeling like this as a mom, but I was also feeling like this in the marriage. We were growing further and further apart. Just going through the motions and detached. I was exhausted, impatient, and falling into a depression. Every night when the girls would finally fall asleep, I would pour myself a glass of wine out of a box, dump some Cheez-Its in a coffee mug, and numb out on the couch in front of the TV, wanting to disappear. Day after day, month after month, year after year.

Lost Control

Having children was the most precious, loving, and selfless act I have ever chosen. This statement is true. It taught me I was capable of loving someone so much it hurt. It taught me I was capable of taking care of another. It taught me patience, understanding and awe. I loved being pregnant and I loved being a mom. I jumped in with both feet and was also left physically and emotionally wiped out.

Being tired quickly opened the door for the seeds and weeds from my past to appear. They had grown such deep roots that the thoughts, doubts, judgments, and criticisms came back with vengeance. I soon began to feel alone, fat, disgusting, and invisible yet again. Although the girls always needed me, something was still missing. I continued to feel empty.

In a moment of confusion and lack of clarity, my husband lost his job. Due to that loss, we also lost health insurance. I was angry, he was angry, and emotional walls formed around both of us. I applied for state health insurance and he fell into a dark depression. There was a distinct period of time where I feared I would come home, and he would be dead. Not only was I angry, but I was also sad, scared, and feeling helpless. I didn't know how to help him or what to do, and I never asked.

Life became out of control. Financial pressure was building and thus my old obsession with weight, food, and body image heightened. Ninety percent of the time, my brain was occupied with calories in and calories out, classes taught and money made. I started teaching more and more and eating more and more. Both became ways to escape. Classes got me out of the house *and* they allowed me to eat more Cheez-its and drink more wine. They became my two essential food groups. Day by day I was drowning, disappearing, and dissolving into a state of emptiness.

So, I Ran...

Ran to another job because we needed the benefits. The pay was lousy, but the benefits were great. I thought that being in a new home, new town, where no one knew us would help too. News flash: *wherever you go, there you are.* The new job, new home, and new surroundings didn't matter. Everything continued to disintegrate. The girls were both struggling, and I was selfishly seeking other ways to be seen.

Step Back:

1. Have you ever done something because you thought it was what you "should do"? Versus what you wanted to do?

2. What decisions have you made to try to escape a situation you were in that you didn't like?

CHAPTER 10

Seeking to be Seen

I kept seeing the ad in a small advertisement every week. It called to me in a way I couldn't explain. This must be what intuition is all about. It popped out of the page, saying, "See me, notice me!" week after week. The thought of it then began to seep into my days. What if I did that? No, I couldn't, but what if I did? I continued to think about it over and over.

Finally, after six full weeks of seeing this ad, I decided to bite the bullet and ask my husband about it. It was a hard subject to broach, but I knew the money part would help. Our relationship had continued to deteriorate, even with the move to this new place, and since money was tight, I gathered up the strength to finally ask.

"Hey, I have seen this ad every week for the past month or so, and it is speaking to me," I said, as I hand the paper to him.

He looked at me and sarcastically said, "Wow, didn't know paper could speak…it never says anything to me."

I rolled my eyes. "Funny," I said, thinking *not really, this would be why it took me over a friggin' month to show it to you.*

"The money could help us right now. I have had easy pregnancies and being a surrogate would make a huge difference for a couple who can't have kids. What do you think?"

"You're kidding, right?"

"No, I'm not, I would like to do it."

He paused and looked down for a serious moment of contemplation. When he looked up, he smiled and said, "OK, sure, why not. Make sure to get the OK from the girls though."

I felt myself filled with joy. I nodded and said, "I will, and… thank you." I lifted my chest and walked proudly away. I was so grateful for his yes. I was going to do something that could make a big difference in the life of someone else. This was different, important, and I would get to be pregnant one more time. I couldn't wait to get started.

Obsession

There was a ton of paperwork to fill out. Doctors' approvals and visits to New York for a series of physical and emotional tests. Then there was the waiting. The waiting for the right person or couple to see my file and think I would be a good fit.

The weeks went by and the waiting continued. I continued to exercise, eat, and drink more and more, trying to suppress the emptiness I was feeling. It felt like I was moving through my days on autopilot. Get up, run, eat, work, drink. Rinse and repeat. Losing days once again due to being preoccupied in my own head and missing the day-to-day details.

The girls were in new schools, and I was there when they got home. One was struggling, the other seemed to be making friends. They both watched a lot of TV and I was watching with them but not always "there."

Yet another year of important memories lost, never to be recalled again. Another decision I made that occupied way too much of my brain. Being able to be a surrogate would make me happy, I just knew it.

Just about the time I was going to give up, the call came in. "Anne? We have a couple that would like to talk to you, are you still interested?"

"Yes, absolutely," I affirmed.

A day later I was on the phone with the couple interested. It was an instantaneous click and the next thing I knew I was on my way to New York to meet them. More tests, more questions, more appointments. Work was great with all of this and the egg transfer happened in the fall of 2007. My uterus home was primed and ready for occupancy. Both eggs loved it. So much so, they decided to stay a full thirty-nine weeks. I worked all the way through, with an awful bout of third trimester morning sickness. Every day, like clockwork, as I was getting ready to take the girls to the bus stop, bingo…in the bathroom I would go. Their dad took them almost every day after that. The twins were born via c-section, over six pounds each, about four months before my forty-fifth birthday.

Before I even could take it all in, it was over. And guess what? It didn't make me happy. All I felt was empty once again. Big surprise. I should have known. I went home from the hospital all alone with only a fat body to show for it. Empty, broken, sad, happy, grateful, and depressed...all at once.

Empty

I sat alone on the couch with the pillow on my stomach and tears running down my face. It was over and I was alone. No one was home and I was stuck here with this body in this dark home. The girls wouldn't be home for hours. The walls continued to close in.

Nine months of glee, nine months of joy, nine months of attention, gone in an instant. With nothing to show for it. Other than a body stretched to hell, no clothes that fit, a scar, and the thought of having to go back to work in this body. Once again, I was flooded with the thought of having to lose weight. I knew everyone at work would be expecting me to lose it right away. Isn't that what fitness people do? Isn't that what is expected of us? All I wanted to do was curl up in a ball, cover my head with a blanket, and pretend I wasn't there. So very empty. This was not what I was expecting.

The weeks passed and I started to be able to move my body. *Finally*, I thought, *it is about time, you fat ass.* I would sit on the spin bike barely pedaling for what seemed like hours.

I cried, slept, and stared at the food in the fridge. Most days I would just stand there staring, with the door wide open. Sometimes I would binge, other times I would go all day without eating.

I would be heading back to work in a week, and I didn't want to go. *What will everyone think? How much will they ask about the babies? Did everyone know I was a surrogate? What if they thought they were mine? What if they start to ask those questions? What if, what if, what if?*

Please God, I prayed, *please don't make me go back. Make this emptiness go away.* There I was, once again, in the empty, dark space that was oh so familiar…

The only thing that kept me present and engaged during this time were the girls. We watched *American Idol* and Nickelodeon at night together. They always filled my cup when they were around. Problem was, they weren't always around. They were teens now and starting to become independent. They were expressing themselves differently and drifting away, the way teens naturally do. At least that was what I felt during this time. As I look back on it, I do believe they tried to engage me more. Tried to get me to play games or do things with them, but I just seemed to always be too tired.

Whenever they weren't around, which felt often, I would spiral into a pool of regret. Wishing I had done so many things differently with them. Wishing I had been more present with them, oh so wishing I could get some of those years back. I fell into frequent spaces of self-pity, self-deprecation, and self-loathing.

I reconnected with that space inside of me, that familiar place, where I just wanted to be noticed and seen. That deep-seated root that continued to yell out, *Notice me, need me, help me feel worthy. I need to feel worthy.*

I journaled for hours on my life and came to the realization of how unhappy I was. The marriage and the man were both not what I had planned for or expected. I realized I was moving through the motions of marriage and faking it for the girls' sake. The emptiness and sadness turned into full-blown disregard and disappointment of the woman I had become. I was taking my own disappointment out on myself in destructive ways. In the only ways I knew. I was binging, restricting, overexercising, and drinking. The medicator of the moment depended on my mood and the environment I was in.

Once I got back to work these feelings eased up. Work distracted me. I made rules up for myself. Do this, don't do that. Easy peasy, I thought.

Being home was a different story. The emptiness and sadness continued to wash over me. As soon as I walked in the door, I would go to the fridge and from there all bets were off. Could be a glass of wine from the "wine box" or a plate full of chicken thighs. Could be a bowl of ice cream, plate of crackers and cheese, or a peanut butter and fluff sandwich. It might be baking a box of brownies and eating all the edges before cutting it into squares. A trick I had been using for years because it would still look like there was a batch of brownies made. All these eating episodes were washed down with a full glass of guilt and shame.

No matter what, I always found something to fill the hole with. Emptiness 10, Me 0.

I found myself back on a "diet" to lose weight yet again after the babies were born. Those months of attention and admiration were gone, and there I was, empty and feeling fat (is fat a feeling even?). It was a dangerous combination.

Step Back

1. Can you recall a time when you felt extreme emptiness, sadness, or loss? When you think back on it, are you able to recall the time before the emptiness or sadness took hold? What was the feeling there? Was it love? Joy? Connection? Emptiness? Grief?

   a. Our pain and sadness are usually closely equivalent to our love and joy. Would you give up the love, joy, connection so that you would not have to feel the pain?

   When I thought about this question, I knew my answer would be to not give up the decision to become a surrogate, even knowing how empty, sad, and depressed I became.

   b. Given the opposition and contrast of joy and pain, how do you respond or react to contrast in your life (hot, cold, good, bad, high, low)?

CHAPTER 11

Destruction

The Start of the End

The surrogacy left me sad, weak, and empty. I thought to myself, *your life is fine, you love your girls, you like your job, get over yourself.* The life I was living was easy to justify. You're fine, so many people would be so grateful to live the life you are living. Suck it up and don't be so self-centered.

And I was disappearing at home in a big way. The relationship between my husband and me felt nonexistent. I was looking for something, seeking something, needing something. The emptiness was just feeling bigger. I started looking for change. Looking deeper inside of myself to see if there was anything in there worth salvaging. The emptiness turned into a yearning, an ache, a desperate need to do something. Something worth doing. Something that would fill that hole. Calm that ache, quench that yearn.

My husband didn't understand what I needed. I didn't

understand what I needed. I just knew something had to give. So I pushed. He pulled. He pushed, I pulled.

I started to pick fights. I brought home a puppy, he brought home a new jeep, neither of us asking the other if it was OK. We started to self-destruct. I complained daily to my friends. Neither of us were happy.

We were breaking apart as a couple right in front of our two teenage girls. I started searching elsewhere to fill the void. I was drinking wine every night and getting up at four in the morning to go running, completely lost. I was spiraling down into my hole and crumbling apart once again.

Surrounded and swallowed up by the circumstances of my own decisions.

Searching for Significance

The crumbling continued day after day. I was searching for anything that would fill me up and help make me feel whole again. One night when I couldn't sleep and it was too early to run, I began to search the internet. I was looking for the next "magic diet" to start. A ritual I had perfected over the years. *If nothing else, losing weight will make me happy.* Down the internet rabbit hole I went. I finally found myself on Facebook. As I was lurking around there, I began to think about people from my past. I found old elementary school classmates, and memories of kickball and sleepovers entered my mind with a welcome smile.

Before I knew it, I was typing in the name of my old college boyfriend. He was actually the first and only boyfriend I ever had before I started dating my husband. I plunged into being a thirty-minute stalker of who he had become. I decided to write him a message to see if he remembered me. I let him know I was married and that I had two wonderful daughters. As soon as I pushed the send button, a fleeting thought came whirling by my brain. *I'm not doing anything wrong right? Because I am married?*

As soon as that thought went through my brain, I knew I was on another seeking mission. I was looking for validation and approval from someone, from anyone. If he remembered me, that would make me feel good, make me feel happy. It was just another choice to try to find external proof I was OK. This might be what could fill up that hole that had been empty for so long. I was searching for excitement, appreciation, acceptance, and joy.

I was living in mom world. Making sure everyone's basic needs were met. Making sure everyone got what they needed and where they needed to go. I was a schedule keeper, appointment maker, form filler outer, driver, cook, dishwasher, and maid. I was a workout maker, problem solver, encourager, supporter, playmate, tear wiper, and more.

And I was empty. The computer seeking had given me a fleeting moment of hope. I stared at the screen. *This is stupid.* I shut the computer down and went to bed.

The next morning, I woke early to an interesting feeling of excitement. Maybe that old college boyfriend wrote me back? I snuck over to the computer and turned it on. There it was. A little red circle in my Facebook messenger staring back at me. A new and different Anne appeared. An old friendship became a new one, blossoming in front of both of us. Our conversations opened my eyes back to myself. Back to the woman I had lost so many years ago. An angel and a cheerleader appeared just when I needed it. He was happily married and shared with his wife our new connection. I said nothing. I assumed that my husband would not get it. I assumed he would get angry, jealous, and take this all the wrong way.

This online connection became the birth of a new "medicator" and a new obsession for me. One that elicited the same high that came from stepping on the scale after losing weight. The same momentary high that came immediately after a binge or a long run. I had found a high that didn't involve food, eating, or exercise. A high I thought was "harmless."

I quickly found myself engulfed and completely consumed with this Facebook relationship. And because of this, I leveled up and heightened my restriction, increased my already high exercise level, and soon spiraled out of control. I was medicated on all cylinders and running on pure adrenaline and numbness. Floating above my life, like a fully fueled addict. Not at all present for the people who mattered most: my girls, my clients, and my family.

It was in the midst of all of this when I discovered the plethora of self-help books and videos out there. While I was floating high, dreaming and wishing, I began sinking my teeth into more and more personal growth. Consumed with fixing myself, so I could make myself better. I had no clue that everything was continuing to crumble underneath me.

Change

We were in the same room but miles apart. He was on the computer while I was on the couch watching a movie my boss had given to me. The movie was *The Shift* by Wayne Dyer. I sat, watched, and cried through the whole movie, realizing I was living my life as a lie. Finally understanding why and how I had completely lost myself. I didn't even know who I was anymore. I also knew I had to make a change.

I stood up at the end of the movie to head to bed, and my husband turned his head toward me and said, "You all fixed now?" in an obvious sarcastic tone.

That tone and those words penetrated me like a knockout punch to the gut. *He just doesn't get it*, I thought. This moment was the beginning of the end. I was not happy, and I wanted more, I needed more, there had to be more. And yet, there I was. *My own decisions have brought me here to right now.* (You made your bed, now sleep in it)

Divine Intervention

I remember the exact moment I knew my marriage was going to end. I had an out-of-body experience, like nothing I ever had before.

I was on the rower at work with a friend and found myself complaining about him (my husband) once again. It wasn't the first time. Complaining about him and our relationship had become a habit for me. The next thing I knew, I looked up and there I was. I was outside myself, giving myself advice.

Again, Anne? Geez… Will you just shit or get off the pot already? How long are you going to have this exact same conversation with yourself before you actually do something? How many years are going to go by that you are still complaining about the exact same thing? What are you going to do? Either get out or stop talking about how bad it is being there!

On that very same afternoon my husband spoke loudly at our oldest daughter about something. The voice and tone cut through me once again. It was too familiar and as I cringed, I knew I was done. Just a few hours ago, I had been told to "shit or get off the pot" by an outside version of myself. Was all this some sort of weird divine intervention? Maybe, and it was also more proof for me. I didn't want to live this way anymore and I wanted more from this life.

Almost exactly two years after the twins were born, we separated, and I filed for divorce. With this one decision, I single-handedly destroyed everything and everyone. At least that is how I felt. I made the choice to leave, because I had lost myself, and my family hated me for it. I didn't blame them either. I hated myself too. This choice to file for divorce quickly fired up my Mini-Me. *You are so stupid, what were you thinking? You deserve to be treated whatever way they treat you.*

Interestingly enough, this decision proved to me that no matter what I did, I was still stuck with my miserable self. The circumstances I was living in continued to mirror how I was feeling about myself. To make matters more confusing, our oldest daughter was being homeschooled due to some bullying in the high school. There was no way she was going back to that school. Our other daughter loved it there and had no intention of leaving, leaving us (my husband and I) with a tough decision. I ended up heading south of the state, and he went north. One daughter went with him to stay in that school, the other daughter with me to enroll in another district.

I was a mess, crying all the time and continuing to run, exercise, eat, and drink. Both girls had pulled away and were trying to make sense of all of this. We hated them being apart, but if they didn't want to attend the same school, we thought this was the best choice.

I made the choice to get off the pot…and was left with the shit.

Perspective Prison

I was still sitting in the prison of my own perspective. My perspective of myself, my body, food, eating, and exercise. From that prison cell, I made choices and decisions that felt congruent with who I thought I was. These choices were blurred by my own judgments and criticisms, keeping me locked inside.

I knew for as long as I continued to see myself as not good enough, all my choices and decisions would follow suit. They fell in line with how much I hated myself. I was continuously trying to change who I was by numbing out my feelings. I was broken, unhappy, and messed up. A perfect example of the self-fulfilling prophecy.

I ran…I drank…I ate…I beat myself up. I snuck out of bed early, laced up my sneakers at three in the morning to head out and burn off all the ice cream and cookies I had devoured the night before. Mile after mile, tear after tear, trying to outrun my own guilt and shame. Which seemed to be chasing after me like a couple of rabid dogs, never leaving me alone.

I could never outrun myself, no matter how many miles I went. The voices in my head were always there, making themselves heard loud and clear. *You have no control, you are so messed up, you are a stupid, fat failure and will never be OK.*

The neighborhood of voices had moved even closer to home, into my bed, and took my brain hostage. They never left me alone.

Never good enough, smart enough, thin enough, strong enough, anything enough.

The voices were so loud and so prominent, I felt like I would never be able to chase them out no matter how far or fast I ran. They all kept right on running right beside me.

I was too afraid to slow down long enough to step out of the open prison door and look at things differently.

Step Back

1. What behaviors do you find yourself reverting to when things get hard, when an external stressor shows up at your door?

2. Have you ever had a "shit or get off the pot" moment? What was it? Did you listen? What did you do?

CHAPTER 12

Addicted

THE STORY I HAVE CONTINUED TO TELL MYSELF IS THAT "I HAVE AN addictive gene." Addicted to food, weight, the scale, exercise, and being seen. Addicted to getting other people's approval, fitting in, and avoiding disappointment. These addictions have helped me avoid uncomfortable feelings. They have contributed to the story I continue to tell myself. The feeling of never being good enough, thin enough, or worthy enough. I have been on a continuous path of seeking approval. From my mother and father to my brother and cousins, from schoolmates and teammates to coaches and teachers.

Always doing things and making decisions to fit in and be liked. I made choices so that others would see me, hear me, and approve of me. As long as I fit in and others approved of me, I wouldn't feel so empty, right? I kept believing their acceptance would fill the hole inside. This hole is the feeling of unworthiness and disappointment I have dug for myself. I have dug it deeper and deeper with the shovel being my own thoughts. My thoughts added fuel to my beliefs and the beliefs skewed the perspective of myself.

This story I have been telling myself, this self-fulfilled prophecy I have been living in, is of my own doing. The early thoughts around not seeming to fit in anywhere, early thoughts of stupid, fat, clumsy. Early thoughts of being different.

I imagine my birth mother's parents (my biological grandparents) must have been disappointed. Disappointed with their daughter's choices and actions. The fact that she was pregnant and unmarried at sixteen was no doubt not what they had imagined for her. It would make sense too that this disappointment had an impact on her own self-esteem. Our parents, after all, are the first people in our lives we want to like us, to love us.

From the seeds I had planted early, I quickly learned I did not want to disappoint my parents. I wanted them to be proud of me. Due to that inner drive, I reacted and responded in ways I thought I should have. If I do *this,* then they will think *that.* Problem is, we have no control over what others will think. All we can do is assume what they will think. I lived my life making assumptions about everyone else's thoughts.

This is where the problem lies: when I did things so others would approve of me (to avoid disappointing them), I was left feeling empty. Leaving myself wide open to count on others to confirm my own worth. I continuously surrendered myself to the thoughts, opinions, and expectations of others.

Lies, Lies, Lies

In order not to disappoint others, I started to lie. I lied so my parents would be proud. I lied so other kids would like me. I even lied to see if I could get away with things. Lying quickly became an intricate part of my story. I got good at telling people what they wanted to hear. Because of this, I doubted myself. I was an imposter. Once again, I had created my own self-fulfilling prophecy. Strengthened the perspective of myself. It allowed me to build an even stronger storyline to live in.

My lying became a way of life as soon as I started dieting. I lied about eating this and not eating that. I lied about exercise and grades. I lied for the protection of my desired outcome: don't disappoint and make sure others like you. I was the kid who told lies to protect herself from getting in trouble (and getting yelled at). In turn I proved to myself I was stupid and no good. The seeds continued to grow deeper and deeper roots.

I lied about who I was with, where I was, what I was doing. I lied directly into the faces of people I love. One time I felt brave and tried to tell the truth to my parents. I got grounded. Proof lying was a better option. Tell them what they want to hear. That always worked.

I was a master at sabotaging myself. I would even lie to *myself* about how much I was eating, how I was behaving, and the decisions I was making. It was much easier to bully myself and talk behind my own back. It helped protect me from being hurt by someone else's words or actions. If I told my parents I was not happy with my marriage a mere year after getting married, I assumed they would have lectured me about my commitment. If I told my husband I was scared he was drinking too much, I assumed he would have lectured about not knowing what I was talking about and to mind my own business. *I am not or will ever be good enough, smart enough, thin enough, pretty enough, talented enough, or creative enough.* So, I lied.

With every lie, I also experienced a surge of energy. An internal feeling of excitement because I had "gotten away with something." The lie enlisted the feel-good hormones dopamine and serotonin. It became yet another addictive cycle, much like eating. Eat, feel good, beat self up, feel bad, eat to feel good again. No wonder the lying became addictive. The lies were lighting up the reward center of the brain. The feeling of being victorious after eating a pan of brownies, and no one ever knowing (until now).

Strengthening my Story

My lies became truths. I had completely convinced myself of my own lies. I had told my lies so many times, I thought my lies were actually truths. They were secrets I chose not to share. *I am fine, I don't have a problem with food. I am not depressed. I don't drink too much, run too much, cry too much. No, I haven't lost weight. Don't worry about me, I'm fine.* The more I told myself this, the more I believed it to be true.

I also began to believe I was a person who keeps secrets. I kept secrets about food, alcohol, and exercise. I made sure I told people what they wanted to hear in order to fit in and be liked. I pretended to be someone I was not and was successful at being deceitful. Damned if I do, damned if I don't.

Every once in a while I would get caught in a lie. When this happened, I had an automatic response: full-blown repulsion of self. My Mini-Me came on strong, filling my stomach with disgust and disdain. She would reiterate that "I told you so" statement. Which was followed by *"See, I told you you shouldn't like me, you shouldn't trust me, that I am a BAD person."*

It was exactly what the inner Annie wanted to be told. *You are not worthy of being liked or being trusted or being anything. You are worthless and can't do anything right.* The story I had chosen for myself. The story of I don't deserve to be happy. The story of I am not good enough (smart enough, thin enough, strong enough, etc.). As long as I continued to tell myself this story, I would continue to make decisions that create the circumstances to support it.

Still Running

When I wasn't lying, I was trying to prove myself. I continued to pursue things and make decisions based solely on what other people would think. *If I take this job, people will think it is cool. If I could lose weight on this diet, people would notice and compliment me. If I compete in this event, people will see how dedicated I am.* I was on a constant quest to find approval and was addicted to it. I needed AA in another sense of the word. I was trapped within my own addictions to approval and to the way I saw myself.

I pursued choices and decisions I thought others would like. Once I got to a point where I knew I would disappoint these same people, I ran. I was terrified of disappointing them. I ran away to avoid it at all costs. I ran away from playing soccer, I ran away from the fire department. I ran away from jobs, towns, and friends. I ran from my ex and from those who loved me. I thought I was running toward the next best thing, the thing that would make others sit up and take notice. The thing that would make me feel worthy and special. Running toward the thing that would fill the empty hole. No matter where I ran, I was left with the same person, *me*. So I continued to run.

I was running to be alone, where I couldn't let anyone else down and where no one could see the real me. I thought I was running to safety. The fact is, no matter where I ran to there I was. Finally, I stopped long enough to realize I was just running away from myself. And I was getting tired of all this running. Tired of all the lies. Tired of trying to be someone I didn't even know. I was a lost soul searching and seeking to find myself.

Belonging

I began to see the empty hole inside of me from a different perspective. It was now feeling more like loneliness as opposed to emptiness. I was seeking outward toward something external to find acceptance and belonging inward for myself. I was yearning to belong.

As I turned inward to face these feelings of loneliness and emptiness, I realized I was not alone. This hunt for belonging is actually part of our DNA. It is both a normal and biological seeking of both children and adults.

Within my search for belonging, I had been changing who I was to fit in with others. I was continuing what I had started in elementary school. Take stock in who I am with, and what is happening, then morph to fit in. I did it to belong to teams, get jobs, or have friends. I re-created myself for whoever I was around at any given time. Always seeking to be seen and to fit in. Feeling "less than" was rooted deep in my story and growing stronger.

I was trying desperately to fit in by making my body look a certain way, yet doing so left me empty and exhausted. It never mattered, because what I was really seeking the whole time was this sense of belonging. Who was I supposed to belong to? The search seemed pointless. I wanted to stop seeking approval outside of myself. No matter what I did to fit in and belong, I still was not happy. Happy was always just outside my reach. Maybe it was because I was looking in the wrong place, outside of me.

Step Back

1. Is it easier to be someone you are not?

2. Who do you seek approval of ? Where do you seek approval?

3. Do you do things for others so that they will like you, or see you?

CHAPTER 13

Lost Moments

THIS PAST WEEKEND, I TRAVELED BACK TO MY HOMETOWN TO ATTEND a "celebration of life" for an elementary school friend of mine. I am not sure what called me back. It might have been the fond memories of dancing to the jukebox in her basement or playing catch in my backyard. An internal feeling and voice called me to go. So I listened to my gut.

I found myself there early. As I drove into town, I was bombarded by memories of my childhood. I drove by the town common where I remember fondly the strawberry festival my parents worked at. Past Gilly's candy store and by the small gas station, where I told my mom I wanted to be a gas lady when I grew up. Down past Emerson's softball fields, smiling as I remember playing my heart out there as my dad coached my teams.

From there I automatically drove out of town toward my childhood home, feeling ever so present with the hills and turns of the roads and houses on the way. The memories came flooding back as I passed the Cannings, the Things, the Hydes, the Ingrahams… and then us. The red door, still there, with the black numbers 206 right above it. The door was the only thing the same though; the house was different. Lots of trees were gone, there was an addition to the left and the basketball hoop on the right was nonexistent. I snapped a couple quick pictures, hoping not to be caught by the homeowner.

I then traveled farther down Perkins Row and over the small bridge where my mom and I would have a picnic lunch after she picked me up from kindergarten. That same kindergarten where I was told I was not allowed to finger-paint anymore.

Just a little farther down the road was the elementary school. The old Stewart School, looking both the same and different. I parked the car and took a walk. I passed the big gym wall where I used to kick a soccer ball for hours when I was in high school. There was now an addition there, prohibiting the kicking of the soccer ball I now keep in my car…bummer. I walked around this new addition to get a glimpse of the playground. The place where kickball, gym class, and recess were my welcome friends in school. As I stared at the newer-style playground, my mind flashed back to the swing set, slide, and teeter-totter of the old days. My tomboy days. I smiled. These were good memories. Life was simple. My weight didn't seem to matter, my body was just my body, and food was just food. I sighed. It was getting late, so I hustled back to my car in my clogs to head over to the church for the memorial.

As I walked in, an old friend saw me right away and gave me a hug. I looked around and recognized a few faces, but no memories came to me. Not at all like only a mere ten minutes ago where I was flooded with vivid memories.

During the service, stories of junior high and high school were shared, and I drew a blank. I could not recall junior high at all. All I could recall was the first day of gym, where I had to put on those stupid tight red shorts. That was it. Nothing until making the soccer team in tenth grade…over three years completely erased from my memory. *Junior high, hmmm. Did I even go?* WOW. There it was, the beginning of the end of my childhood memories….

It wasn't just those three years though now. There are multiple months and years over the last forty years that have disappeared from my memory. Times when my brain was only filled with the day's numbers. Filled by the obsession around the weight on the scale. Memories missed due to the calculations of calories in and calories out, miles run, and sit-ups counted. Memories of meals eaten, meals missed, and food both hidden for later and secretly thrown away.

Times where I was there physically, but not emotionally. So many memories lost because I was obsessed with my body size and what I looked like. Always trying hard to either be seen, or to hide, depending on what the number on the scale said. And due to what I did or didn't eat that day. The almighty scale, which dictated my mood, my worth, my actions, and behaviors year in and year out. No wonder I don't even own one anymore. When was the last time? I can't even recall.

Years in every decade, gone. Experiences missed, because I didn't want to be seen, because I thought I was too fat. Wanting to disappear because I knew everyone would notice how much weight I gained. Knowing that everyone would whisper to each other how I used to look so much better.

Memories of sitting at family gatherings, staring at the food table. Not even knowing who else was in the room or attending. Years of staying in the kitchen, doing dishes and secretly eating that one brownie left on the plate...or one more spoonful of mashed potatoes.

I sat in that church listening to my former classmates talk about school so fondly. And I had missed it. Missed much of college, missed much of my first couple jobs, missed time with my girls growing up. All because I was consumed by my own appearance and hatred of self. Hatred, such a strong word, yet it fits so perfectly to the emotions I recall starting that first day of gym in junior high. That day I had to ask for a larger size pair of shorts. Over a forty-year struggle hating my body and myself... and missing out on life.

I don't want you or anyone else to have to live this way. You don't need to miss out on experiences, relationships, and memories, being consumed by the size and shape of your body. Or because you feel you are unable to trust yourself around food. Or that you feel you are unworthy to have a seat at the table. All because society, family, and friends believe that you should look and act a certain way.

I want you to know that you are so much more than the size of your body. So much more...

Step Back

1. What have you missed out on or said no to because you were worried about how you look or the size of your body?

PART III
WEEDING

CHAPTER 14

Sandboxes

THE EVENT POPPED UP ON MY FACEBOOK FEED. PUSH-UPS FOR Charity to benefit the Wounded Warriors. It was sponsored by a guy I had gone to college with. He owned a business called To Be a Champion, specializing in sports performance and fitness. We both were phys ed majors. I remembered him as being smart, funny, and kind. His name was Tim. I thought it was a good cause and I loved push-ups. Of course I did; I was still in the midst of my compulsive exercise. I was running all the time and had just decided to sign up for my first half-marathon. I was working in the fitness center at a New Hampshire college and thought it might be fun to compete with him. New Hampshire against Maine to see which state could do the most push-ups and raise the most money.

After exchanging a few messages and emails, he asked to meet. He had the certificates, registration, and liability forms to give to me. We decided to meet at a restaurant about halfway between us to talk about it and so he could give me all the paperwork. What I remembered was right: he was smart, brilliant actually, funny, kind, and cute too. We talked all through lunch. He listened closely to me with pure interest and curiosity. Not an ounce of judgment. This was refreshing. I was relaxed, open, and honest. He was not trying to impress me, I liked that. He was just being present and caring. I was comfortable and felt calm, connected, and was captivated by him. I liked him. It could have been perfect, but it was way too soon after the divorce. I was not ready for this and I knew it was not a good idea to get involved. I was still broken, fragile, unsure, and unstable. The girls were still angry at me, confused and sad. Yet, I still found myself thinking about him...

At the end of our meeting, he asked if he could see me again. "I'll think about it," I said. And I did. As a matter of fact, I couldn't stop thinking about him the rest of the day. There was something different about him. A softness, a sensitivity, a lightness. And then there was his kind heart, quick wit (like my mom's), and intelligence (like my dad's).

After giving it a lot of thought, I called him and asked if he would come up to New Hampshire and analyze my running gait I had my first half-marathon coming up and I knew he would be able to help. Seemed innocent enough right?

That meeting sealed the deal for me. This was worth it. Tim made me feel special, calm, relaxed, and even smart. I continued to say yes to seeing him again...and again...and again. His attention, assurance, and authenticity made me want to be around him more and more.

Even though I was still broken, unstable, and unsure, I knew this was something special. I also knew I had to set up some boundaries, because if I didn't, it would not end well at all for either of us.

On our third date I told him straight out: I didn't need fixing, even though I knew I was broken. I didn't need someone judging what and when I ate, what I drank, how much I exercised, my weight, or my body. Those were all my business. Not his. End of discussion.

The words hung in the air. I don't need you to fix me, my behavior and body and are off the table. They are mine to figure out and deal with. Not yours or anyone else's. I waited for him to head for the exit sign. He didn't. He just nodded and smiled. He heard me and I felt heard, he saw me and I felt seen, he understood me, and I felt safe. Until I wasn't.

Call for Help

He was living in Maine; I was in New Hampshire. We continued to date, seeing each other every week or two. Growing closer and closer. Open, honest discussions, long walks, and lazy afternoons watching movies. It was about eight or so months later when things started to unravel. I was still in the cycle of restriction, overeating, and overexercising, and he didn't really know because I was able to hide it from him. We were apart weeks at a time. It wasn't until he started to stay with me longer that he began seeing my destructive behavior.

Although he didn't actually say anything, I could see the disappointment in his face. He would shake his head when he saw me exercising for the second time that day. I could see the judgmental looks and the disappointment in his face when I got up to get another glass of wine.

If I wanted this relationship to work, I knew I needed some reinforcements. Especially if I wanted to be able to sustain my own boundaries. My immediate reaction was to withdraw and run away. Just go, it was easier than trying to figure all this out. So, I tried. I tried to call it quits and broke his heart. Interestingly enough, I ended up breaking mine too. Something inside of me, during this space of pain, made me pause long enough to reach out for the help I knew I needed.

I was sitting at the small beach in Sunapee, New Hampshire, journaling about my confusion and brokenness. (Journaling has been my best friend ever since I was pregnant with the twins.) Without hesitation, I picked up my phone and googled addiction therapists. There were two nearby. I called one and there was no answer and no answering machine. I took that as a sign. One more to try, so called and left a message. Within the hour, my phone rang, and I made an appointment for later that same week.

My "therapist in my pocket" (what I now call her) enters my story here. I was in need of help, advice, and support, and my teacher had arrived. She is my mentor and confidant to this day. I spent the next couple of months with her trying to figure out why I was so broken, so scared, so fragile, so stupid. As I dove into the work on myself, I knew I wanted to bring Tim in to be a part of it. This therapist could help us move through this journey together in a healthy way.

He was ready and willing to go with me and hear what she had to say. I sat in awe as she put into words what I had wanted to yet was unable to. She spoke it all in a way that Tim could hear and understand.

She let both of us know we could not control what the other person does, how they think or how they behave. We could not control how each of us would respond to specific situations. The more we actually try to push our own agendas onto each other, the more the other will push away. The more he tried to convince me his thoughts and opinions were right, the quicker I was going to head in the other direction, and fast. I was ready to run, once again.

Until I was given my own sandbox.

The Sandbox Moment

This wonderful therapist stared at him and watched his eyes filled with tears as he realized I was destructing right in front of him. Just my way of proving to him that I wasn't good enough for him…

I sat there thinking, *see, I told you I am broken, that I suck and that you want no part of a relationship with me.*

"This is her stuff, not yours," she said to him.

"Yes, but I want to help, I love her," he answered.

"Yes, and this is hers to do what she wants with," she replied.

"I don't need fixing," I interject strongly. And in the next breath, without even skipping a beat, I hear myself saying, "I am sorry, I won't do it anymore," and I lower my head in shame.

"This is her sandbox," she says.

We both look at her. "What?"

"You both control what you do with your lives. You do many things together and are in a relationship and you also have individual personas. There are things you both do and want to do that may not be great for your health or well-being, but you do them anyway. These things are you playing in your own individual sandbox. The other person can see that you are numbing out or hurting yourself and because they love you and don't want you to do it, they try to help. They jump into your sandbox."

She continues. "The problem with this is that the other person does not want to be fixed or helped at all. It is just like the teenager who begins to date someone you don't approve of. As soon as you tell them they can't see them anymore, what do they do? They sneak off behind your back! That is what they do, saying to themselves, 'Don't tell me what I can and can't do!' (cue hands on hips). They are declaring their autonomy.

"So, when it comes to food, exercise, or alcohol for Annie, she may feel she needs to sneak it because she knows you may judge her and be disappointed in her. She knows you do not approve of what she is doing and want to help, thus all the more reason to sneak it."

Yes, yes, yes! That's it!

She continues, "Respect each other's sandboxes. The more you try to jump into the other person's sandbox, the more resentment will build up and the more the unwanted activity will continue to happen. Stay in your own sandbox. The only exception is, when you decide you want to invite someone into your sandbox for some help."

Wow-zah…have sandboxes completely changed my life!

The sandbox theory is a polite way to say to someone you love, "Stay out of my business. This is mine, not yours."

I had been hiding the drinking, eating, and exercising from him for months now. I continued to exercise without his knowledge because I didn't want him to worry about me. I would drink and hide it because I didn't want him to worry about me. I would lie about food because I didn't want him to worry about me.

The even deeper reason was, I didn't want to disappoint him.

Disappointment was a seed I hadn't realized, or maybe just forgotten about. It connects with the stupid Sally seed. The one planted every time I broke something, did something wrong, or made a mistake. Deeply rooted with the numerous disappointing looks of my parents. To me, disappointment meant failure, disappointment meant not good enough, disappointment meant self-loathing. Disappointment felt like abandonment. Disappointing someone hurt me the most. I think disappointment was actually my biggest fear.

I didn't want to be a disappointment to Tim because that would prove I was not good enough for him. This realization, and having my own sandbox, changed things.

Due to this sandbox theory a new belief and understanding was born. The truth is that I *will* disappoint him, just as I have disappointed my parents, my daughters, and myself. Being disappointed is part of human existence and experience. It sucks, yet it doesn't define you, your worth, or your value. It just becomes another teacher. You can disappoint me, and I can still love you. I can disappoint you and still be loved by you. I can be a disappointment and still make a difference. I can show disappointing behavior and still be of value.

It all comes down to owning a different perspective around disappointment. And around disappointing yourself and others.

Annie's Sandbox

My eating, my exercising, my drinking, my body were all mine. They were all placed in my own sandbox. They were not his. Period. Unless I invited him in and asked him for help. He had his sandbox items and I had mine. If he began to jump into my sandbox, I was able to let him know, "This is my sandbox." It became a gentle and playful way of saying "none of your f'ing business," and I loved that.

I continue to share this "sandbox theory" with my clients who are in need of setting boundaries. They are now able to put their weight, their food, and their bodies into their own sandboxes with great success. It has allowed them time to heal their relationships with food and body. They have been provided space without the judgment of others, without the "helpful suggestions," without the sarcastic comments, without the disappointing looks. Pure brilliance.

Step Back

1. What pushes your boundaries and heightens your feelings of anxiety and fear (the fight-flight-freeze response)? What subjects trigger you into running away, numbing out or fighting?

2. What are your sandbox boundaries with the people you love?

3. How can you set up your own sandbox?

CHAPTER 14.5

Love on the Rocks

It just happened. I did not want it to happen, but it did. I tried to control it, but I couldn't. I remember the specific moment I fell in love even though I was fighting against it. The ink barely felt dry from my divorce. Not yet…it was too soon! It didn't seem to matter; time and time again he proved to me that he was the most caring, sincere, patient, and kind person I had ever been with. And that was just the beginning of what attracted me to him. That part was his brilliance, passion, drive, and dedication to his work, his friends, and his family.

As we stood on the pebble beach at Fort Williams in Maine, looking out at the expansive ocean before us, he wrapped his arms around my waist. We could feel the cool breeze across our faces, and the contrasting warmth of the sun. He whispered in my ear, "Close your eyes and listen. What do you hear?" I closed my eyes and wondered what he was talking about; all I could hear was his breath, the soothing rhythm of the ocean waves, and my Mini-Me saying, *"Listen harder, you're not doing it right."* I was confused and unclear about what he was getting at. He sensed this and continued, "Don't think, just listen. Listen to the sound of the rocks as the water travels through them on their way in and especially on the way out." I listened closer this time…mmmm…mesmerizing, relaxing, soulful.

The waves crashed over the rocks with an energizing force and sound. And as they retreated, you could actually hear how they soften and glide gently back to their home, making the most wonderful sound. It reminded me of the sound of maracas being played softly in the distance. I was at complete peace, for the first time in years. I had complete trust in this man. The love came from a place deep inside. It cannot be forced. It cannot be timed. It comes when we least expect it. Too soon? Who knows? All I knew was, this felt right. Oh, so right.

Third Time's a Charm

He asked me to marry him, I said no. Too soon, I am not ready. He said, that's fine, I just want to let you know I will keep asking, once a year. I raised my eyebrows and gave him that "Ya, right. In your dreams, I don't think so" look. Well, I was wrong. This man is now my husband and every day I learn more about him and fall more and more in love with all of him. He is my biggest fan. His love and support have stabilized my foundation. He makes me want to be a better person, and I do that for him too.

CHAPTER 15

Tipping Point

IT'S THREE P.M. I AM HUNGRY, MY STOMACH IS EMPTY AND GROWLING. The last thing I ate was a salad at five last night. I am feeling frustrated, anxious, and perturbed. Let's get on with this so I can get on with my life, so I can keep on running, jumping, teaching, moving.

The hospital bed is uncomfortable, and I am antsy. I've been lying here all day, waiting to get wheeled into surgery for my knee. I am so proud and excited to have made this decision. This surgery will allow me to get back to running, teaching, and working out. It will allow me to keep exercising and pushing my body without so much pain.

Over the last few years, my knee has made it hard to continue to work as a fitness professional without pain. It has been hard to hold on to that oh-so-important "fit-pro" image I have worked my whole life for. This persona is the only way I have ever been seen. It is what is expected of me. And lately, I have had to live not being able to do the things I have always done. I've had lecture after lecture from doctors to stop. Stop running, stop jumping, stop pounding.

Ya, right. What they all don't know is that exercise has been my life. It has defined who I am. It is the only way I know how to be. I *have* to be able to run, jump, and teach. (It also is the only way I know to stay in control of my weight.) The surgery today is going to put me back on track. It'll allow me to keep being me.

The doc comes in minutes before wheeling me into the operating room. He has his green scrubs on and looks tired. I am his fifth knee surgery of the day. Last on the list, due to the complexity of the surgery.

He greets Tim and me and apologizes for the wait. He casually states, "I wanted to let you know that if I get there and your knee looks too bad, I won't be able to do this surgery. Because no matter what I do, your knee would still give you problems. We will have to discuss a knee replacement instead."

I stare at him with a blank, confused look, my insides knot up and the internal voice in my head fires up: *WHAT??? Are you fucking kidding me??? You're not going to be able to do this? Thanks for nothing, doc. Why have you not said this before? Why am I just now learning about this?*

My brain malfunctioned, what did he say? Did he just tell me there is a possibility that I won't be able to live my life the way I am supposed to? *Ummm, NO thank you.* This is not acceptable, period.

A fake smile spreads across my face and I say politely, "OK, thank you," because that is the way I have been taught to respond:

Suck it up, just say OK, yes that's fine, I will do that, you're right, I'm sorry, I was wrong, whatever you say. Appeasing, accepting, and allowing life to happen to me, as if I do not have a voice. Complying, conceding, and obeying. Being kind, considerate, and thankful, that is how I am supposed to be. All the while completely ignoring the soft little voice inside that is scared and sad.

The doc turns around, pushes the draped white screen aside, and leaves the room. I turn to my husband with tears in my eyes and want to say with certainty, "He's not going to be able to do the surgery." But instead, I mumble it, almost as if to make sure I can say it out loud.

I know this for sure. I know my knee is too bad. I know he won't be able to fix me. My eyes continue to tear. My Mini-Me kicks in. *What am I even doing here? Why have I been so stupid.... again? Why didn't I realize this was all just a pipe dream? What are my parents going to think? How am I ever going to explain this at work? How am I going to keep my weight down?*

I already know before the stretcher even starts to roll, the life I had planned for myself is history. What the hell am I going to do now? I have spent so much time and brain power planning on this. So much so my future was counting on it. I quickly start to see my life destruct and crumble right in front of me.

I turn and manage to say to that loving man who sits by my side, "He won't be able to do the surgery." I have tears running down my face.

He hears me and knows. I can tell he feels my pain. I see compassion, love, and understanding begin to radiate from him. It is because of this look, this unconditional love, that I know deep inside that everything will be OK.

Unexpectedly, a sense of peace and calm washes over me and enters my heart. I feel a relief of sorts. Somewhere in my head a soft voice is saying, *thank goodness, we finally have an excuse to rest. This body is tired, we need rest, it is time for us to rest.* This is proof my knee really is messed up. A reason I do not have to keep beating on it just to prove to myself. A wave of warmth flows over me. Maybe I can finally stop trying to be who others think I should be?

I close my eyes for a moment and the tears subside. I see a space in the audience of my life, right there in the front row, off to the right. There are only a precious few people sitting there. As soon as I look at them, I feel safe, protected, and worthy, no matter what happens next.

I had no idea this section even existed. I have only seen the rest of the audience. The proving section. You know the place, where all you do is continue to try to prove to everyone else that you are who they think you are? The section where they all know and approve of you and what you are doing because you have made sure of it. You have made decisions and acted in the way you thought you should be in order to be seen, liked, and accepted by them.

I close my eyes, feeling my stomach growl yet again. This time, it feels different. I notice it is my own physiological hunger, and I smile. For the first time, I am *not* thinking, *oh, good I am hungry, maybe I'm losing weight.* I am listening with a more compassionate heart. My body is telling me it would like some food.

Well then, I guess I should start feeding it. In that instant I hear from my heart, from my gut, and from my whole body. It says to me:

THANK GOD! Finally! Yes, allowing us to rest would be a wonderful thing. Feeding us would be even better. This body is tired, really tired, please let us rest…allow us the chance to share with you who you are. You are so much more than your body. Please know it is just a small part of you. Rest, dear Anne, Rest.

For so long, the search for the lock on the escape hatch of my thoughts and feelings has been picked by different keys. Keys of punishment, food restriction, overexercise. Picked by Mr. Atkins, Jenny Craig, Judge Judy, Perfectionist Patty, and more. The control of calories in and calories out. The manipulation of my body by the punishment of exercise. The stuffing of food, the drowning in alcohol. The distraction of attention, the lies and false decisions. All to be seen and noticed.

I have held myself hostage in this prison I made to protect myself from pain and disappointment. To protect myself from rejection, from hatred, from embarrassment and humiliation. Medicating and escaping from my uncomfortable negative feelings for so long. And in doing so, without realizing it I have been blocking out the good ones too. I have been running from all feelings. I have been running from myself. Mile after mile, trying to outrun or chase after the desired thoughts or emotions I thought I was missing out on.

As I sit waiting, I think about how interesting it is to look at your own story with a fresh new perspective. To finally realize that you have been sitting inside your own prison. A prison that you created by yourself, for yourself. It takes sharing this new perspective with someone else to finally get hit over your own head with the realization that you are not alone. What is most interesting is that the door to this prison is wide open. It has never even needed a key.

Light Dawns

Light dawns on Marblehead is a phrase my mom used to say. I can choose to continue to sit here and try to escape and run from my feelings and thoughts. Or I can choose to step out the door of my prison to find what's awaiting me. I can find out what it's like to experience these emotions and feelings I have been avoiding and numbing out. I can find out what it is like to experience the joys and sorrows and the ups and downs. I can embrace the anger, the grief, and the heartache. I can enjoy the excitement, the connection, the beauty, and the revelations. I have the ability and the choice to quiet all the voices that are not me: my parents, coaches, friends, and society. I do not have to be who *I think,* **they think,** I should be.

The choice has become mine, if I choose to take it.

It is time to till the garden and replant some different seeds. Plant truer seeds of me and not get so tangled up in the weeds that have taken over from the seeds of the past. I have been living in the weeds of my mind. I have owned and acted upon the beliefs I planted long ago. All of a sudden, I realize I can choose to think… see…act…and live differently.

Time to Shit

The time has come to move through my own shit. I have come to a space and time where I'm tired. I'm tired of living within so many stories, labels, and identities. I'm tired of being someone that I am not. Tired of choosing to own these stories as mine. Tired of calling myself names and owning old identities.

It is no wonder I have continued to live a disillusioned life. I have created my own self-fulfilling prophecy.

- I have told myself that I am a "runner": I run away from things when they get hard.

- That I am a liar and am dishonest.

- Believed I am always looking for attention.

- Believed that I am a fraud, an imposter.

- Believed that being in a smaller body was the only way to be seen, valued, noticed, happy, worthy, or successful.

- Believed that happiness came only to those who looked a certain way.

It is time to pause now and weed the garden of my seeds, stories, and identities. It is time to choose differently. Time to break up with the identities of old. Break up and mourn the tomboy, the athlete, the runner, the fit one, the dieter.

I am making a decision to love and accept that I don't know where I came from. To love the fact my birth mother had the resilience to go through the pregnancy to have me. To accept that I may not have been wanted by her but was desperately wanted by my parents. To accept that I don't know who took care of me for the first few months of my life and that I have no idea who my birth father is. I can think of myself as *given away* as a gift or *thrown away* as trash. The choice is up to me. *And* the fact is, it doesn't define who I am right now. It does not mean I am not worthy or garbage. I am writing a new story for myself. It means I am here to fulfill something, to make a difference and to provide hope. That is what I choose to be my new destiny, my new story.

By accepting and understanding, my past discretions and lies are just that…they are in the past. I can choose to believe they protected and helped me and that I am a different person now.

I have lived and learned a lot from my experiences. I have heard they call that wisdom. Wisdom comes when you open your heart to learn from your experience. Wisdom is sitting in a space where you can look at your experiences and see them with a new perspective. Allowing you to gain understanding and knowledge from them. If you don't take the time to do that, they may become experiences that define you. Truth is, they have nothing to do with right here and right now.

What would it look like if I decided to step into this life and unlock my wisdom? What if I finally dropped all the baggage I have dumped on myself and been carrying around all this time? It may look a lot like this:

The following is the prayer I wrote, the day after getting home from the hospital, where I did not have surgery, because yes, my knee was too bad.

Dear God, (my belief system of a higher power)

I am so sorry for all the pain I have caused others through my actions. I am sorry that I have sidestepped my inner gut and have been weak. Sorry I have turned to food, alcohol, exercise, and distraction to disappear from myself. Sorry I did not let myself feel the pain, disappointment, and sadness within me. I am ready now to feel, forgive, and release. I ask of you to forgive me my sins...my failures...my dishonesty. Please guide me and help me see myself the way you see me. I know it is only you who sees all of me, who knows everything, who has watched me self-destruct. I need and want your support, your love, your guidance, and your forgiveness. As I pray this to you, God, please allow me to trust and be open to it. I am willing to accept your unconditional love, forgiveness, and guidance. I am open to the possibilities. I am willing to step into me, into this Annie that stands before you today, in all her brokenness and all her glory. Please guide my heart, my words, and my actions.

Let me see a different perspective on this amazing journey through the world that you have given me. Amen

Step Back:

1. Do you know the real you? And can you describe that?

2. What are your false identities?

3. What false identities are no longer yours to hold on to?

CHAPTER 16

Tired

As I recovered from my *non-knee surgery*, I took some inventory.

I thought about how many times in my life I have looked in the mirror and told myself I need to lose weight and go on a diet. I should do this, I need to do that, I have to stop doing this. Over and over again. It is like I can't even hear myself anymore. I have been holding so tightly to the belief that being thinner will make me more likeable. That being thinner will make me happy. That being thinner will make everything OK. All these beliefs have been on an automatic replay loop.

Sitting in the hospital, hungry and waiting to have the doctor "fix" me, was the first time I paused long enough to hear and be aware of the harsh voices in my head. I was able to notice these voices were all outside of me. It was the first time I had the wherewithal to pause long enough to question them. It was a tipping point.

The "losing weight" voice was just a cover-up to something deeper underneath. It was the weeds of the garden. The roots were something different altogether. By only seeing this perspective around my body, I had only heard those particular voices. It was the group of voices I had recruited that continued to strengthen my thoughts. These roots sprouted identities. These identities of myself became my story. My perspective. The story of how I lived my life.

It is within this awareness I decided to rearrange this "neighborhood" full of voices in my head. The voices like Stupid Sally, Captain Criticism, and You're a fat pig Paula. I was not going to continue to listen to the voices that fueled my addiction to food, exercise, and alcohol. And to be honest, I was realizing they were no longer working for me. They were no longer motivating me. I was too used to their harshness. Used to following their every word. I did not want them to be comfortable anymore. I did not want to *choose* to continue to listen to them. They were chains holding me down.

In these moments of pause and nonjudgmental curiosity, I became aware that I had a choice. A choice to either continue to fall back to old thoughts and behaviors or to change them. I had the choice to move out the neighbors I had rented so much space to or move to a new neighborhood myself. The awareness of my own perspective was my aha moment. "Ahhh, light dawns on Marblehead." What might my thoughts even be if I wasn't thinking about weight, exercise, food, and all that is wrong with me?

Once I was able to see these repeated thoughts, behaviors, and beliefs, I was able to look at them all differently. I became curious around them. Actually, realizing that my thoughts and beliefs had been standing in my way. My thoughts symbolized and protected the beliefs of my past, not my future. They had been making decisions for me and, in turn, sabotaging me.

I realized I had the ability to make conscious, different choices.

As soon as I became aware of hearing a familiar voice in my head, I would pause. It gave me the ability to hear it through a new filter. I noticed how often the same self-talk or the same conversation with a friend appeared. No wonder I continued to run. With the newfound ability to pause, I was able to step back from it and see it differently. This enabled me to come up with different thoughts so I could make different choices. The awareness elicits a pause in thought and allows a slowdown in the automatic negative self-talk. I call it a speed bump. A purposeful slow-down of the automatic self-flagellating.

The speed bump has allowed me time to ask myself different questions. Questions like:

Is continuing to beat myself up, lie, restrict, binge, run, and drink the way I want to continue to live my life? Do I like the way it makes me feel? What is the end goal here? To be thin? To be appreciated? To be liked? *And then what? And then what happens?* Because it has never worked before! Whenever I think I land at my end goal, nothing has changed so I just run away anyway. And then I start the cycle all over again.

Asking different questions led to even more questions. Which led to more weeding of the garden. Where did all these voices in my head come from? Why do I believe the things I do about myself? Who told me this was what I was supposed to think? Where did I learn them and why are they so strong?

Groundhog Day

I was living in the movie *Groundhog Day*. Every year I spent dieting, restricting, overexercising, and putting on weight. Every year I was searching for the answer, beating myself up for binging or not staying on a diet. Year after year feeling like a failure. Never fitting in, never being happy. I was also left with years of missed memories with my kids. I was tired. So tired of beating myself up, exercising, and feeling deprived. Tired of always searching for the next answer to all my problems through weight loss. Tired of blaming my body for everything that was wrong with me. Tired of pinching my thighs, yelling at myself, running myself into the ground. Tired of the thousands of sit-ups, tired of the lying. Tired of feeling stupid because I couldn't figure this shit out, like everyone else seemed to have. Just plain tired of listening to the replay in my brain and hearing myself complain over and over again. Tired of seeking outside of me for the answer that would never be there.

I was done. If I truly wanted a different result, I would have to do something different. I would have to stop looking outside of myself. Stop seeking approval from everyone else. It was time to start looking inside to myself. It was time to be more compassionate and curious rather than judgmental and jealous.

I saw things differently the moment I accepted that I had been looking in the wrong place. I was looking in the bedroom for the recipe book that has always been kept in the kitchen. I started to question what I had always done and shift my perspective around it. Seeing it from a completely different vantage point gave me permission to choose to think differently. Permission to choose to rest. This permission to choose provided me with a pause that was followed by a wave of calm. A wave of peacefulness that comforted me like a warm blanket.

It was *that one choice to accept myself* at the weight I am and to stop searching for the next thing that was going to (or supposed to) make me happy. That one choice to start questioning the way I was living and the beliefs I was living by. It was time to admit I had been wrong. I had to admit I had been lying to myself and holding on to false beliefs. I had to admit that my behavior had repeatedly hurt others. I had to admit I was blaming others for my own actions. It was time to take responsibility for myself and my actions, thoughts, and behaviors. I also had to admit that even when I did lose weight and look like I thought I was "supposed" to, nothing changed. I had years of experience to prove that.

Yuck. Did I actually have enough strength to start from scratch? To start the process of rethinking, replanting, and re-believing?

The comfortable and easy choice would be to keep thinking the way I had. Keep falling back on and relying on my old story. Believing what I had been told to be true about who I was and about the size of my body. It would be easy, convenient, and comfortable to continue to listen to the old neighborhood voices in my head. The easy choice. The familiar choice. The comfortable choice. Yet, if I decided to follow the easy and familiar choices, it would keep me stuck right here in this same place. I would be right here in this space next year at this time and the year after that, and the year after that. My choice, easy? Or hard?

I decided the easy choices had run their course.

Imagine, all it took was that *one* awareness, and *one* decision to free myself. One hard choice to take that first step outside the door of the prison in my head I had been keeping myself in.

One scary-as-hell choice.

I chose to reset my beliefs. That all these voices and people in my head were not actually me or mine. They were all just the thoughts that had been planted long ago. They have repeatedly shown up during periods of my life. They have shown up when I was stressed, overwhelmed, and scared, and they have helped me avoid pain and disappointment that I was not strong enough to face. For this, I am grateful for these voices; they have served a purpose up until now. So today, I am choosing to honor them and then move them across town. Much further than I had ever let them go.

I could have made the choice to keep believing, choosing, and thinking the same things (while expecting different results), or I could choose to step into the unknown and get different results. I was choosing to step into the fear of not knowing what that different result actually might be.

You, too, have the ability to choose something different. Becoming aware that you have this choice is the first step.

Notice when you continue to have the same thoughts over and

over again. As those familiar thoughts come into your brain, they are magnetically attached to more similar thoughts. Thus, leading you to the same behaviors and actions. The only way to change the outcome is to break this chain of thought somewhere along the line.

The awareness of the unsupportive thought allows you to pause and step back. It allows you to see it from a different perspective and allows you to opt for a different thought. Different thoughts lead to different behaviors and actions. I was aware my thoughts of *you're a fat, lazy slob, and need to lose weight* every time I looked in the mirror were only sabotaging my decisions. This one thought would lead to a new diet, more exercise, a glass of wine, or a binge. As soon as I made the choice to stop, pause, and choose a different thought, I was empowered. A different thought was followed by a different choice, a different behavior…

Beliefs Sprout from Seeds.

My story…from Annie Fannie Farmer, to husky, to watch what she eats, were all seeds of thought. These seeds rooted thoughts, beliefs, and the perspectives of myself I perceived to be true. *I am fat, must lose weight, diet, succeed, fail, hate self, eat, I am fat, must lose weight, diet, succeed, fail, yadda yadda…*

The thoughts then triggered my behaviors. Both the thought and the behavior were then repeated…over and over again. Making it a habit. The habit became the story I told myself. It became my identity and who I thought I was. Before I even knew it, the self-fulfilling prophecy was born.

Just the other day, I was trying on some jeans. They were too tight. Instantly, I was back in that Sears store, trying on pants. Mini-Me pops in: "See, told you." I breathe. I close my eyes. I see the ten-year-old Annie in the mirror. She does not need to hear these harsh words. She needs a hug. Compassion. Validation that she is OK…just as she is. Those are the thoughts I hold on to. Those are the words I choose.

It is my choice if I decide to hold on to my old identity or change it. All depending on what I want to feel and how I want to live.

Side note: There is a strong tendency to choose what you have always chosen. The comfortable and familiar. Deciding to make different choices leaves you with a feeling of uncertainty. Different choices are scary. Period.

Are you willing to decide to be scared, decide it's worth it, and decide to make a different choice?

Remember, the definition of insanity:
Same choice = same result.
Different choice = different result.

Step Back

1. What belief or behavior is taking up time and energy in your head? Are you willing to notice and willing to try to see a different perspective?

2. When I started to ask different questions, the phrase that came to my mind was "shit or get off the pot." This

phrase has kicked me in the ass so many times. It was this exact thought that gave me the courage to leave an unhappy marriage. It was this exact thought that helped me make the proclamation that I will never diet again. It was that thought that had me pick up this computer to start writing this book: ***What is it time for you to shit or get off the pot around or about?***

CHAPTER 17

Spiderwebs

Triggers are Teachers

I wonder what high school and college would have been like if I weren't always trying to fit in with other people. I usually agreed with others, in hopes they would like me. People pleasing, self-criticism, and judgment paved my way forward. It allowed me to find connections with others. When I felt resistance or disagreement with someone, I would beat myself up, assuming it was my fault. No one else could be causing this resistance, must be me. Blaming and trying to fix myself became the norm. My mind was screaming to *"please just keep the peace. Don't disappoint, don't speak up, don't question."*

I made comfortable choices to fit in and the more I did, the emptier I felt. I now had the opportunity to make another choice. Was I willing to choose to release this need to fit in with what others think or want? Ugh! How? I don't even know what I want or what I think.

Although I did know now that making the same choice has led me to the same outcome. I was tired of the outcome I was getting. So, *I made the hard choice.*

Whenever I come up against conflict with people now, I step back, pause, and ask the question: What are they trying to teach me right now? People who trigger me into reaction are teachers for me. They push me to look deeper into myself. I'm able to see my interactions from a compassionate and nonjudgmental space. A space that makes room for questioning my thoughts and the willingness to think differently.

"You have to try meditating! It is the best way to connect deeper to yourself. It quiets your mind and enables you to feel more peaceful, calmer, and make better decisions! You have to try it!" I kept hearing this over and over again, from teachers, therapists, and self-help books. I had continued to hear how meditation was the only way to truly connect to yourself. I tried and tried and tried to sit with myself to no avail. My brain continued on a hyperspace thought train. Always going a mile a minute, no matter how hard I tried to "focus on my breath." Mini-Me was ecstatic! *See...told you. Why bother even trying, you can't do this...focus, connect, pause? Ya, right, good luck with that! Why would you think you could sit and be with yourself? You don't even like yourself!*

There must be a way I can do this; I can't be the only one who has a hard time focusing and sitting still. I decided to reach into my pocket and call my therapist. She recommended I listen to some talks by Kyle Cease. He had a different way of thinking about meditation altogether. I soon began a new journey with another mentor.

"Just sit back and watch the show of your mind," Kyle said. "Just allow your mind to entertain you." Hmmm. I can do that. For the first time, I began to spend some quiet time with myself. All I did was watch my thoughts like I was sitting in the front row of a movie theater. I noticed my feelings without judgment. I heard Mini-Me's harsh words yet did not attach myself to them. I began to create some distance between her and me. It was a completely different way to experience meditation. I liked being able to *allow the chaos* rather than try to silence it.

As I continued to meditate this way, I began to experience some deeper feelings. I noticed a deeper sadness and grief of how I was living my life. I experienced a profound sense of forgiveness and gratitude for others. Tears would stream down my face on a daily basis. I allowed myself to sit in the experiences my mind wanted to share with me. It was fast and furious some days and slow and calm others. I let go of expectations and welcomed each new meditative experience.

As I sat back, I became the witness to my own thoughts. It was in this state I realized that my thoughts were just thoughts and they didn't have to define me. I didn't need to hold on to them and continue to build a network of more and more thoughts around them. I had the ability to shift my thoughts. I could build a new network of thought to support me, rather than beat me down. I would visualize my thoughts as birds flying around in my brain. They were separate from me.

My thoughts began to fascinate me. Did you know that we have thousands of thoughts a day? And more than half negative! We actually learn to choose certain ones over others to focus on and hold on to, due to our experiences. Not only that, but over eighty-five percent of the thoughts we have are repeated day after day.

I used to grab onto a thought and think it was cast in stone; it was who I was or what I was. My thought was me. My thought was true. I visualized the thought as one of those birds stopping to make a nest and move in. Just like my Mini-Me has! Mini-Me built a beautiful retreat nest in my brain. She moved in with all her friends too. They have been having a wonderful time hanging out and sharing their thoughts with me.

This network of thoughts and beliefs have defined who I am and defined my identity. They all sprouted from the seeds I planted in the garden of my mind. All those childhood seeds developed deep-rooted thoughts. They have since infiltrated my mind with weeds. They have been responsible for what I think about myself and who I think I am. They have dictated my thoughts, guided my actions, and controlled my beliefs.

A single thought of feeling uncomfortable in a pair of pants or one look in the mirror would spiral my brain into negative Mini-Me thoughts. It would soon magnetically attach to a network of corresponding thoughts. When this happened, I would find myself focusing even more on those thoughts. The thoughts became grander, louder, and more aggressive. They ended up spiraling me down deeper and deeper into an abyss of self-destruction. All it would take would be a funny look from someone. Mini-Me's destructive, degrading words would come at me loud and clear.

It was only during my meditations I was able to see these thoughts from this different perspective. I was able to step back and widen the lens. Within this perspective I continued to see they are not my truth. They were automatic thoughts that have found themselves caught in the spiderweb in my brain. It was like a magnetic pull attracted more and more of the same destructive thoughts to the party. Seeing it from this place and space, I realized I was holding myself captive. The spider (Mini-Me) had caught me in her web. And I have become very comfortable there.

The thoughts of self-deprecation, self-hatred, self-judgment, and self-criticism were easy. It is no wonder I have continued to get caught here. I am good at it! So good in fact, I have lived my life believing these thoughts cannot be changed. They are true facts. They are who I am. They are me. Period.

Your Spiderweb

This spiderweb of thought has been built over many years. All the thoughts we thought when we were kids have formed pathways in our brain. Our brain knows them well. They are well-worn, much like the path you took through the woods to your friend's house. You traveled it so many times, it became more and more open, well-worn, and traveled. So open in fact, that the city could have come in and paved it. It is no wonder the brain becomes attracted to these thoughts. Anytime anything closely resembles a similar thought, another one comes jumping in.

Particular thoughts have been deeply entrenched in the soil of your brain. On both sides of this path there are weeds, bushes, trees, and brush. So the path becomes the thought of least resistance. In order to shift and change your thoughts, you have to step off the path and into the weeds and brush. This stepping out into the weeds sure doesn't feel very good. It is uncomfortable. It is much more comfortable to stay on the well-worn path. It is easier, more familiar, *and* you have become very good at it.

Once you are aware of this, it puts you in the position to make a choice. Think the same thoughts, end up with the same behaviors, actions, and outcomes. Think different thoughts, have different behaviors, actions, and outcomes. Yes, but…this is hard, this is uncomfortable, this is scary! Yes, and…this can change how you see yourself.

The truth of the matter is that I am not my thoughts. You are not your thoughts. It must be true, because there are times in our lives where we have changed our thoughts. We have changed how we feel about things. I used to hate reading, hate crime shows, and hate history. I used to hate dresses, brussels sprouts, and washing my face. There were times I felt happy and was not thinking about how fat, stupid, and unworthy I felt.

I have been using my thoughts and beliefs about myself as a mask. As a costume and coat of armor. Protecting myself from the "real world." Protecting myself from getting hurt, from being disappointed, from being different. I have been so busy fighting to fit in and trying to be like everyone else I have kept myself stuck. I have kept myself from experiencing what was happening around me because I have been walking back and forth on all the old pathways.

I have followed these paths, used these words, and kept these thoughts to keep myself safe. They have kept me from feeling proud, successful, loved, and appreciated. I have dismissed compliments and brushed off congratulations. All for the right to stay dismissive, to stay depressed, sad, angry, and feel unworthy.

This intricate magnetic spiderweb of my own thoughts and feelings has defined me and the way I live my life. They have been the biggest part of who I am, and they are leftover thoughts and beliefs from my five-to-fourteen-year-old Annie.

Realizing you have the ability to choose to believe something different is empowering. Once you understand that you can make a different choice, you can see a different perspective, the way you see yourself changes. This awareness allows thoughts to float in and out. We can both allow and give permission to sit and be there with them. We can do that without letting ourselves get magnetically pulled into the spiderweb of our own self-destruction. You can choose to notice, accept, and allow the thoughts to move through your spiderweb and not get stuck on replay.

The work comes in when I see if I can stay true to my new choice. Will I be able to hear someone make a comment about me, my weight, or my body and not allow it to penetrate me? Will I be willing to tell myself that it is just *their* perception of me? Thus, I don't have to own it as mine? The answer is up to me, it is my choice. My answer has always been the same; now it is different. My answer now is yes.

This body is my home, it houses my mind, soul, and spirit. It is my choice how I get to feel and think about it. And so do you.

Step Back

1. What pathways have you built in your brain?

2. Can you identify your triggers?

3. If you were going to step into the weeds, what words might you say to yourself?

CHAPTER 18

Challenging Thoughts

Have you ever noticed the feeling in your body that takes hold the moment someone says something to you? Especially when the words hold a specific tone? Or maybe they say something that threatens your self-worth? Our circumstances and experiences with the outside world draw us back into our old thought patterns.

The other day, a client's spouse said to her son, "Just a small slice of cake for Mom," and before she even knew it, she felt like she was punched in the gut. Her mind connected to all the other thoughts and feelings those words brought up. It connected to her mother's words, to her grandmother's words, and her ballet teacher's words.

These are instantaneous thoughts and physical sensations that we have no control over. The mind and the body are intricately connected. The magnetic spiderweb of thoughts seems to ignite the body's response. Or is it the other way around? Is it the body's response that ignites the magnetic spiderweb of thought? Because it feels instantaneous, kind of like the chicken or the egg dilemma. It is amazing how all our old stories (and identities) get connected and enmeshed together. All it takes is a few simple words, a look, or a tone of voice.

As soon as her brain heard the words, *bam,* those familiar voices and thoughts flooded in. Her mind connected like a magnet to past experiences. It connected to feelings, emotions, memories, thoughts, judgments, and comparisons as well.

"Just a small slice for Mom" becomes *I am so fat, he hates how I look, he is disappointed in me. Why can't I control myself, I am such a failure.* These thoughts fire up our internal defensive mode: *how dare he say that to me! Who does he think he is, I'll show you what a small slice of cake is…*

This woman's mind was overconsumed with these negative thoughts. So much so that it drowned out everything else, so she missed out on the experience.

It is within these experiences where we find ourselves losing moments. We forget conversations and lose memories due to the self-absorbed addiction to our minds. Due to our racing thoughts and obsessions. We become engrossed, imprisoned, and preoccupied within ourselves.

Releasing or letting go of this magnetic pull is one of the hardest things to break. It feels like we need to get a big old machine and do a full-on tilling of the thought garden. A weeding of the seeds and roots of beliefs that were planted long ago. They have been watered, strengthened, and rooted into the soft matter of your brain. They have also created paved, comfortable pathways throughout.

Soon you begin to notice how strong the old stories are. Mini-Me's beliefs and thoughts come from the interpretation of past experiences. By noticing an old thought and neutralizing it, you can ignite a disconnection to it. It can lead to a separation of this magnetic spiderweb. It will eventually lead to a decrease in the strength of these negative thought storms over time.

"The Work"

Our thoughts have become like superhighways in our brain. They started out in childhood as small pathways. But they now have had years of wear and tear, years of overuse. Just like that pathway I made from my house to our neighbors. Year after year, I ran back and forth. My thoughts of myself had become automatic.

As soon as I started to question my thoughts, I started to wonder about where they came from. Wondering, also, how they had become so strong and automatic. Whenever I am in need of answers now, I reach out and ask for help. I was turned toward a new teacher. This time it was Byron Katie.

Her "four question" model from "The Work" was the help I needed. It gave me permission to question my thoughts even more. This was where I learned how much power I was giving my thoughts. All the thoughts I had about my body contributed to strengthen my beliefs about my body. Thus, my thoughts and beliefs around food, eating, and exercise too. Katie's four questions opened up a whole new way of thinking for me. It allowed me even more choice. It helped me see the path, the patterns, and the perspectives I was stuck in and continued to choose, kept me depressed, isolated, embarrassed, and ashamed. As I stepped back to get a bigger view, I could blaze a whole new path for myself. One that would alter the way I thought of myself, thus shifting my beliefs and behaviors.

If you believe you are fat, your brain will associate and attach more thoughts to support that belief. If you believe you are strong, your brain will connect to and support that belief. Period. It is just the way our brains work. I always figured my thoughts were a fixed part of me. So, when I had thoughts that felt wrong, I beat myself up for having them. These thoughts triggered emotions that felt wrong too. There was always anger because I had "eaten a bag of cookies" or "missed a workout." There was jealousy because a friend ran a marathon, or someone lost twenty pounds. Along with humiliation and shame because I couldn't fit into the pants in my closet or stick to a diet.

I had no idea I had the power to look at all these thoughts differently. As I did more of the "work," I realized my *well-worn* thoughts assisted in keeping me thinking the same way. They kept me stuck in the prison of my brain walking back and forth on the pathways. They kept me from seeing that the door was unlocked (on the other side of the weeds), begging me to walk out.

Having the ability to step back from a thought and say, "Hmmm, here is another interesting thought I am having. I can hear you. Thanks for sharing. You have been helpful in the past, but for today, I am going to choose another thought," I began weeding my brain of old thoughts and old beliefs.

The Thought Train

See if you can follow my brain here. I think this thought:

"I don't want to go to Thanksgiving dinner tomorrow. I hate going, everyone is going to see me, judge me, and watch what I eat" *Next instantaneous thought that follows is:* "I shouldn't be thinking that." *Then flies in* "I should want to go, I should want to see everyone." *Next thought:* "Why am I so selfish?" *Next thought:* "I can't believe how you don't even want to go see your family! You are so selfish!" *Next thought:* "You are such a loser; you should be ashamed of yourself," and so on. The thought storm spiral. The brain getting caught in the spiderweb of thought. Just the one thought that you think you shouldn't have had sends you down the rabbit hole.

A thought storm spiral usually takes one of three paths. Path A: You beat yourself up for thinking that way. B. You find yourself justifying thinking the thought. Or Path C: Both Path A Path B. You find yourself getting swallowed up by your thoughts and have gotten yourself "caught" in the web.

What I learned from both my therapist and Byron Katie was that having a thought does not mean you are good or bad or right or wrong for having it. It also means that you are having the thought for a reason and you have the ability not to attach yourself to it. Remember? Our thoughts become teachers. We can learn from our thoughts, yet do not have to attach to them.

As I practiced seeing my thoughts as just thoughts, no more, no less, I was able to release my attachment and judgment of them. It became easier to live in the present moment. I was able to release the fear, worry, and anxiety that followed self-degrading thoughts. I was able to wipe away the old spiderwebs. Doing this separated me from the pain, isolation, and sadness I was living in.

I said yes to the invite to go kayaking. I hadn't seen my college friends in years. I was nervous because my body was different than it had always been. Remember? I was the fit one, the dedicated one, the strong one. My Mini-Me kept popping into my head as I drove toward the lake. *They're going to think…they are going to be…how can I face them looking so different?* All of a sudden, I caught myself in mid-self-criticism. Isn't this exactly what I am learning? OK, so now what?

I took a deep breath and said to my Mini-Me, "Thanks for sharing, that is not helpful right now." They all have no idea the way I have lived my life. They don't know how much I have struggled with this. This is a great opportunity to practice stepping into the uncomfortable weeds. Allow the thoughts in (birds fly in), notice them, and then allow them to fly right out. Focus instead on the water, the kayaking, the conversation. Don't focus on your body or their reactions. Focus on fun, connection, laughter. I uncomfortably said that over and over again.

There are many ways to learn to allow thoughts to move through you. Unfortunately, the process of doing this is usually uncomfortable. It feels unfamiliar and foreign, and for this reason, it is truly a practice.

My thoughts like "I am fat, I am stupid, I am clumsy, and I can't do anything right" led me to living a particular way. Thinking "I never say the right thing, I'm so stupid, I am a loser, I can't control myself" have keep me stuck. Which contributed to me making particular decisions. These decisions led to circumstances. The life I am living now. This is due to the neural superhighway in the brain, which has now linked to my own self-fulfilling prophecy.

I am responsible for my life as it is right now. Unless you make a conscious decision to question, change, or release your thoughts, you will continue to believe your thoughts are you.

If you have the same thoughts day after day, your behaviors stay the same day after day. This reinforces more of those same thoughts (thus the same actions and behaviors). When I made a choice to believe that my thoughts did not define me and gave myself permission to question them, they no longer had the ability to dictate my life.

Think for a moment about your behaviors (because they are connected to your thoughts). Are your behaviors supporting you? If so, keep thinking the same thoughts. Are your behaviors sabotaging you? Are they hurting you? If so, know that you have the ability to shift your thoughts.

New Jeans

When I used to visit my parents, I would walk into their apartment and immediately feel like a little kid again. Not wanting to say the wrong thing or screw up. These feelings quickly revert my brain back to all my old thought patterns and old feelings. This is all within seconds and without my parents doing or saying anything! I immediately would start to feel judged and take on the energy of that judgment. Because of this, I tightened up and did not act like myself. I believed whatever thoughts came up. Even though no one has done anything to justify them. I made the decision to assume it and take it on. As soon as I do, I give them all the power and feel five years old again. Crazy...

Now, I make a conscious (and still uncomfortable) decision to shift my thinking. To realize I am not five anymore. To know I can act and think in a way that is true and authentic to me. I don't need to follow my old pattern of thoughts. I don't need to assume the worst.

Those thoughts of being a fat, clumsy, stupid failure kept me stuck in the old patterns of dieting, restricting, and overexercising. And believing the only way others (and my parents) would like me was if I were thinner. If I were more disciplined, smarter, better.

Why are these old thoughts comfortable and familiar? Because they have a lot of training. Old thoughts are Mini-Me thoughts. My Mini-Me has been training a long time with these thoughts. Day in and day out. No wonder Mini-Me is so strong.

Making the decision to shift my thoughts has been hard. Just the thought of trying to train a new voice was overwhelming. I knew I needed to recruit some friends and supporters into my brain. The problem was that none of them had any training. So, they had no idea what to do or say. They needed some breaking-in time.

Choosing new supportive thoughts is kinda like putting on a new pair of jeans. At first, they are uncomfortable, a little stiff, and don't feel quite right. But in time they begin to feel cozy and familiar. They begin to move with you, are comfortable, and you actually find yourself feeling really good in them.

The thing is, you won't know what life will be like in the new jeans if you don't spend any time breaking them in. The more time you spend in those jeans, and with your new thoughts, the more comfortable they will become. The good news? Those new and different thoughts also end up eliciting new and different behaviors.

Once we begin to value ourselves, our behaviors begin to change. When you start thinking of yourself as having value, you will also start taking care of yourself more. It is time to recruit another voice in your brain to help you experiment with your thoughts.

Step Back

1. Are you able at this point to pause, step back, and look at your thoughts from a different perspective?

2. Are they keeping you stuck and confined in the same self-destructive patterns?

3. Are you finding yourself continuing with behaviors that are associated with old thoughts?

CHAPTER 19

Choosing to Replant

WHEN I BECAME AWARE OF THESE PATTERNS OF BEHAVIORS THAt were repeating in my life, I decided to look at the common denominator. Me. This scared the crap out of me. Now that I knew I had the ability to make a different choice, I also realized there would be a different consequence, of which I knew nothing about!

For me, it was worth taking the chance. I was ready to take the step forward in the dark, not knowing what was next. I was sick and tired of living the way I was living. I was ready for a different outcome. I was ready to weed through the stories I was telling myself.

I quickly became aware that this choice thing was going to be challenging. I always thought when it was time to make a choice it was either this or that. I have always seen only two choices: Say yes, or say no. Eat something good or eat something bad, go for a run or take a nap. Much like the book series: Eat this, not that. A wonderful example of black and white thinking. Right or wrong thinking. All or nothing thinking.

It was time to step into some "shades of gray," because it is never just this or that. What I have found to be true is that our choices don't have to be black or white. There is a whole continuum of choices in between. These are the shades of gray. It was time to step away from the black, away from the white, and find a compromise in the middle. As I did this, all of a sudden there were many choices in front of me.

Weeding the old, planting the new.

Choice 1: I could choose to say the same comfortable things to myself. I could continue the same dialogue and continue to make the same choices. Choices to support weight loss, to support the thin ideal, and to support my thought *"I am fat and stupid."* If I hold on to this belief, I will move about my day in that exact frame of mind. I will make choices to support this feeling, this belief, this story. If I believe I am a fat, stupid slob, I will make sure to prove that to myself through my actions. I will also elicit the help of the neighborhood friends in my head. As we know by now, they have a lot of practice keeping this dialogue going all day.

With the dialogue of "fat and stupid" repeated through my brain, I continued to seek out diet plans and workout programs. I spent hours trying to figure out what I should do next. My brain was constantly overloaded and in "fix myself" mentality, leaving no time to think about anything else.

Choice 2: I could say "fuck it" and step into behaviors that support this thought. The thought that it doesn't matter what I eat, what I do, or what I look like. No matter what I do, I will always be and feel this way, so I might as well eat whatever I want and give up. I can choose to numb out in front of the TV, with a box of cookies or carton of ice cream, and let it ride. Problem with this choice? Well, it would lead me back to choice one. That has been the story I have lived. The Diet to Fuck It to Diet Food Plan is deeply rooted in my brain. It is the path of least resistance.

For over four decades, I have been stuck in the cycle of going from choice one to choice two, with nothing to show for it. I am like a monkey swinging from one tree to another, back and forth, not going anywhere.

I put on my new, stiff jeans and start to dig into the roots in my brain. There needs to be a way to find choices that are different than this. I pause for a moment and look down. What kind of jeans am I wearing? Men's? Women's? New? Old? Ripped? Stone washed? Blue? Straight leg? Boot leg? Our choices are much like jeans.

Choices 3, 4, and 5: I could start the day differently by choosing to release the thought of losing weight. I could throw away my scale and never step on it again. I could allow my body to let me know how I feel.

Choices 6, 7, and 8: I could start the day with some self-compassion and gratitude toward myself. I could become vigilant and aware of the voices that want to pull me back into old thought patterns. I could push the pause button on them and try to talk to myself differently. I could give myself permission to actually ask myself what I want and what I need. Asking myself what might feel good or make me smile.

Choices 9 and 10: I could choose to accept my body as my natural and perfectly imperfect home. I could *actually decide* that it is OK just as it is. I could decide to fuel it, move it, and take care of it in a way that is supportive, kind, and even joyful. I could choose to look in the mirror, smile and say hi, thanks for being here, instead of something else.

The Peanut Gallery

I have the opportunity every day to make a choice on how I see myself. It is important for me to remember I have many choices. It is not black or white, this or that. I realize they will feel unfamiliar and uncomfortable until I have broken them in. I have to be willing to choose a different path over and over again. I actually have to make the choice that I am tired of the choices I have been making. They have created this life I have been living. And I can choose to not live this way anymore.

The hard part here is that when I started to think differently, fear and uncertainty showed up big and bold. I began to think about all the unknown possibilities. This elicited the peanut gallery in my head that pops up to make sure I know how idiotic a different choice is (this peanut gallery, as I call it has been programmed to make sure you hear you are crazy to think a new thought might be good for you).

Hard truth: The moment I forced in a compassionate thought a whole new audience of voices started in. This peanut gallery started to share all their thoughts with me. Thoughts like:

Who do you think you are? What are other people going to think? People will think you're conceited and "all that." You don't deserve to be kind, happy, silly, relaxed, content!

It was easy to listen to these voices and agree with them. Yes, you are right. Where do I get off having the right to be nice to myself? I don't deserve that. The peanut gallery was pushing me right back into my comfortable Mini-Me voice. If I have a choice to adjust and shift my Mini-Me voice, can I also choose not to listen to the peanut gallery? What if, "peanut gallery," I decide not to listen to your questions, concerns, or thoughts? What if I decide you might not know what is best for me? What if, maybe I do deserve to be happy? Silly? Content? What if?

Awareness Changes Everything

The noticing of a specific thought, action, or behavior brings up an internal voice. It shares with you what you are noticing. Whose voice is that? What are they saying? Are they afraid? Uncertain? Angry? Are they feeling shame or guilt? Are they afraid of being embarrassed? By opening up a nonjudgmental space to hear (and validate) the voices in your head, the voices begin to shift. The tone of the voices starts to soften. They're trying to tell me something! What is it they are trying to tell me?

When my old Mini-Me voices come a-calling, I now use this visualization:

I close my eyes and envision a five-year-old me, leaning up against one of those old oak trees in the backyard (the ones that outline the football field, remember?). She is crying, sad, and beating herself up (her Mini-Me is on fire). A grown-up me comes over to sit next to her and leans against the tree too. This grown-up me gives little me permission to feel whatever it is she is feeling, validating it without judgment. By allowing all the feelings, allowing her to be sad and to cry, these voices quiet down. They don't have as much power.

This visualization started to help me find some new ways of thinking about myself and talking to myself. I started with some fact-finding around new concepts: appreciation and gratitude.

My thinking began to shift. Mini-Me and friends were not so loud anymore. A peacefulness started to grow inside. Whenever those old familiar thoughts came in, I would first acknowledge them. I would then proceed to hear them, affirm and validate them. Then, I would shift them. Some of my newer thoughts were just facts. Facts like.... *My body likes fresh air, my body likes to walk, I am a kind person, I am doing the best I can. My body feels good with nutritious food, my body likes ice cream, I like ice cream, it's OK for me to like ice cream!*

This shift in thought was followed by a change in my attitude and behavior.

One of the best things I did was to develop a *go-to thought*. Whenever Mini-Me and her friends started to voice their harsh and degrading opinions, I would say, "Thanks for sharing," in an honest and heartfelt tone. Those three words started the process of hearing and validating them. I made sure my tone was authentic and real. I became appreciative of the thought. That one pause of validation was followed by this: "I'm going to choose to think this instead today." Other thoughts might be, "I'm human, I am doing the best I can, I'm OK, that's just an old thought, that is not helpful right now." The key is to give yourself the opportunity to pause and shift the thought.

I also found that if I stood up a little straighter and smiled, my new thoughts became even more potent. These two physical actions help to increase the body's physiological relaxation response. Endorphins (serotonin and dopamine—the feel-good hormones) are released, and stress is lowered. For me, these actions turned into an increase in my self-confidence while I was relearning. One thought at a time.

Note: The body's physical actions can help elicit different emotional responses. Standing up straight, smiling, laughing, and taking a deep breath can all help to shift your internal state. The physiological shift brings about a boost in confidence.

I thought about the prison my thoughts had been keeping me in. I had the key all the time. The simple act of awareness changed everything. Awareness that I had choices I call my "Ruby Red Shoe" moment, like Dorothy had in *The Wizard of Oz*. Repeating the same thoughts, planted by seeds so long ago, were not working. I had been listening to and believing all the voices in my head for far too long. My awareness and validation, along with the questioning and inquiry (nonjudgmental curiosity), were the first steps to recover from my own low self-worth, self-esteem, and self-hatred.

There are unknown possibilities, and they are staying the same. You have the key to your own prison, and you are wearing the red ruby shoes. Your choice.

Awareness of Happiness

Trying to seek happiness from someone else is the same as seeking anger from someone else. Happiness is an inside job. Being happy comes from within. By relying on someone else to make you happy, you put a lot of pressure on them and take the pressure and responsibility off you.

Notice the language we use. *She makes me happy; he makes me angry; she frustrates me; he makes me feel loved.* Interestingly enough, many times the same person who "made me happy" also "made me mad." The same person who "frustrated" me also "made me laugh." Think about those words from a different perspective for a minute. "*Makes you.*" My mom used to "make me" go outside. My coach used to "make me" run sprints. Old bosses used to "make me" finish projects on time. Are other people responsible for "making you" feel something? And if so, how is it they actually do that?

How I felt with other people has much more to do with how I felt inside about myself. If you are angry over an argument, what is your response when someone cuts you off in traffic? What if you are feeling full of zen from a yoga class? What is your response then? One minute a certain look from my husband might make me smile. In the next minute, that same look could make me shake my head in frustration. It all has to do with what is going on *inside me* at any given moment. Here is the big takeaway: We get to choose how to respond, always. I knew for me, it was time to let others off the hook and take responsibility for myself.

I always thought happiness, peace, joy, and contentment came from outside of us. I thought it was something we did for someone else or was happening around us that got a specific response. I thought it came from looking a certain way. From belonging with a certain group, from being in a relationship with a certain someone. I thought it came from accomplishing something amazing or weighing a certain number. Yet none of these things ever made me happy. I have years of proof. Nothing ever consistently made me happy. Not a certain weight on the scale, a certain size on my jeans, a "stable" job, or another glass of wine. I was never content, never peaceful, and always striving, pushing, working.

Hard truth: It is no one's job to make you feel a certain way. Knowing you have the ability to cultivate your own happiness, peace, joy, and contentment is terrifying. It means taking responsibility for your own feelings, choices, and behaviors. It means believing that you are wearing the Ruby Red Shoes.

Step Back

1. How do your thoughts make you feel about yourself? (This is my interpretation of Byron Katie's "Work.")
   a. What emotions bubble up with a particular thought? What memories come up?
   b. When you feel that way, what behaviors follow? How do you treat yourself?
      i. What is the outcome of having that thought? Who would you be without that thought?

    ii. What might be a different thought?

    iii. How does this thought make you feel?

2. What is keeping you stuck in Oz, when you would like to be somewhere else?

PART IV
REPLANT

CHAPTER 20

Planting New Seeds

The Mini-Me Bully

Every time I looked down at my legs, my Mini-Me would begin her assault. She has been programmed over and over for the past forty years. She had lots of ammunition and lots of experience. She knows exactly what to say easily and efficiently. Mini-Me repeats the phrases of the past.

Entire days have been taken up with comments and criticism from this internal Mini-Me. She's counted calories in foods and calculated exercise hours. She has blamed, shamed, and guilted me into decisions around what and how much I should eat. As a result of all this internal chatter, I would end up so frustrated and angry. *I'll show you,* I would think and end up heading to the kitchen to binge on whatever I could find just to quiet her down.

I finally became sick of listening to myself! Over and over again, the same thoughts and dialogue continued. With *no change* in thoughts or behaviors at all. Spending a lot of time, money, and energy to stay exactly the same.

The way I was talking to myself, thinking, and acting had become automatic. My behaviors were automatic too. I would start thinking fat, and spiral into eat, stupid, run, shame, drink. Rinse and repeat. All in the name of trying to get out of my own head. The only way I knew how to do this was to eat less, move more, and preach about it along the way. Stupid. Think stupid, eat, think fat, run, think not good enough, drink. I was at war with myself, bullying myself daily.

Brené Brown would say I had become both the bully and the bullied. It is no wonder the whole bullying thing hit such a chord with me. Anytime I felt bullied, witnessed bullying, or heard about someone being bullied, my body would heat up. Anger would fester. Lashing out would occur. The day my daughter came home in tears due to being bullied at school, I was ready to take on anyone who got in my way. I now realize it was because I was one of the biggest bullies of them all. It was time for me to engage in an inner battle with my Mini-Me, with my inner bully.

Hiring Maxi-Me

It was time for a new leader to come into the neighborhood and put Mini-Me in her place. Time to create a more compassionate, empathetic, and stronger alter ego to stand up against my Mini-Me.

I wanted to take a different look at my own inner bully. As I began looking at all the voices (friends) she had recruited over the years, I knew it was time to challenge her. She was not helpful to me anymore. Nor was she protecting me. All she was doing was blocking me from feeling, experiencing, and living. She was keeping me stuck and was keeping me running, both at the same time. She knows the language, knows the tone, she knows the buttons to push. The only way to slow her down is to give her some competition and challenge her. If you want a different result, you have to do something different. I decided to engage another voice. One that was supportive, strong, kind, and compassionate.

This thought of being kind to myself was terrifying. Why would I not want to listen to these voices who have been with me forever? They have been motivating me, haven't they? Who would I be without these particular thoughts and voices? How would I be able to function without them? I don't know if I am strong enough to let them go; I don't know who I will be if I let them go. These negative voices have had so much practice doing what they do best. It seems impossible to tell them the race has been cancelled and they are no longer welcome to compete for my worth.

So, there it was. I could stay hanging out with my old friends expecting different results, or I could decide to step away from them. It was time to replant new seeds.

Maxi-Me Plants her Seed

Step right up, Maxi-Me! Maxi-Me is the voice in my head I created to help me out of the self-destructive neighborhood I had created for myself. Maxi had some things to learn though. At first, she had no idea what to say or what to do. I had to supply her with some ammunition and training. It was like when you try to learn something. Whether it's dribbling a basketball, reading a compass, or writing your first paper, it takes practice and preparation to learn it, get better at it, and internalize it. And even more practice to become good at it.

Maxi-Me was a newbie, a rookie; she had no training at all. She had only been given little snippets of ammo from time to time. When she did speak up in the past, she was blasted out of my brain by a much more powerful army of thoughts from Mini-Me and her friends.

Maxi-Me and I were in for some hard work, some uncomfortableness and frustration. It would have been much easier (and much less effort) to revert back to the old Mini-Me thoughts. But I was determined to stick with this hard choice. So, Maxi and I were relentless. We continuously searched for words and phrases to neutralize Mini or to at least quiet her down a bit.

The broken record that Mini-Me had been playing was old and worn out. I knew that as long as the words stayed the same, so would the results. If I wanted to live differently and feel different, I would have to think differently. The only solution I knew was to recruit new thoughts, phrases, and words for myself. It was the only way things could start changing.

As Maxi-Me continued to get more information and ammunition, things began to change. I supplied her with new words and thoughts to help her out. I was taking her to the positive self-talk gym every day and she was getting stronger and stronger. I could sense Mini-Me was getting tired of fighting this new, strong, and educated Maxi-Me. As Maxi continued to win some rounds, she began to feel strong, confident, and energized. The tired and defeated Mini-Me started hanging out on the couch and napping.

Part of Maxi-Me's routine was pushing the play button on a self-talk audio made through the Self Talk institute. My husband, Tim, had recently become certified as a self- talk trainer (by Dr. Shad Helmstetter) shortly after my knee surgery. He started playing these audios in the background as we were getting ready for work, eating breakfast, or cooking dinner. To be honest, I thought it was silly. How can having this stuff playing help someone start to think more positively? But whatever. I loved him and it didn't bother me, because I didn't even have to listen.

Before I knew it though, things in my life started to shift. I began not to hear Mini as much and I started to feel more confident in myself. I started to make different choices and decisions. I started to stand up for myself and create boundaries. The proof was in my thoughts and my behavior. I was changing. What was different? I was aware that my Mini-Me was stealing moments from me and I was listening to strengthening words around me and feeding Maxi-Me.

As Tim continued to share with me what he had learned, I became more curious. He was another teacher placed in my journey. He shared how we learned to talk as toddlers was by listening to the words and phrases that were repeated around us. We learn to talk to ourselves from the way others talk to themselves and from our experiences. If we are put in places where we are surrounded by positive, strong, and compassionate words, those words become part of our vocabulary. If not, then they don't. It is the simple law of repetition.

My Mini-Me developed from my surroundings. From other people's words, phrases, beliefs, and behaviors. It is no wonder she has been hanging around so long. By surrounding myself with positive words and phrases, thinking differently became easier. Maxi-Me now had her playbook and was doing her reps at the gym.

This new positive self-talk gave me hope, power, and independence from my badgering, bullying Mini-Me. Tim helped me uncover this Maxi-Me who had been living inside all along. It has allowed me to give her a fighting chance. With this Maxi-Me by my side, I knew I was capable of seeing myself differently.

The time had come to move out some of the people who were living in the neighborhood home of my head. They'd overstayed their welcome and it was time for new friends. So I found new friends and moved out the old. The old friends live down the street and visit now and then. They pop in to make sure I really don't want to have them move back in. Sometimes I engage them in conversation and other times I don't. It always depends on how well I am actually taking care of myself. How tired I am, how stressed or how engaged in my life I am. If I am stressed, tired, lonely, hungry or angry, Mini-Me has a much better chance to hang around for a while.

Maxi-Me needed some help so she rounded up a group of friends who are now mine. Some of my new friends include: Accepting Abbe (my legs carried me a long way today; these pants are really comfortable; I am going to the beach, wearing this bathing suit, and going in the water), Confident Callie (I know I will be able to ask my boss for help; I got this; I am strong; I've worked really hard on this), Joyful Jackie (this feels so good; this tastes so yummy; I deserve to be happy), and Playful Polly (let's swing on the swing! I don't care what they think! Dancing feels so good!). These new friends live all around me. They give me space and come when I call them. They help me shift my perspective on many things. Especially on how I see my body, how I move my body and how I fuel and take care of my body. They also help me realize that I am worthy of loving, laughing, living, and more. They have brought peace, freedom, and joy into my life, and have given me much hope for the future.

Step Back

1. How has your Mini-Me protected you?

2. Are you ready to enlist a Maxi-Me to help you too?

3. Is it time to release and move out some of your self-talk "friends"? Even though they may be the most comfortable friends you have.

Your choice. Hold on to them? Or find some new friends? Is it time you gather yourself a new team of supporters and encouragers that allow you to shift your own perspective on how you see and think of yourself?

CHAPTER 21

Willing

Hope

I now have hope within this journey I have led of self-hatred. I was willing to take a hold of this hope and turn it into action. I was willing to make different choices because I did not want to continue to live in this story. With Maxi by my side, I felt hopeful I could find a confident, comfortable, and content relationship with myself. I felt hopeful I could have a relationship with food that would be freeing, fun, and fueling. I felt hopeful I could develop a relationship with my body that was respectful, accepting, and appreciative.

As I started to think differently, I also started to look at my life from a different perspective. It was time to accept and own the lies I had conditioned and programmed myself to tell. It was from this new perspective I was able to see my past actions with more clarity.

I knew step one had to be forgiving myself and declaring a truce on my body. I had spent my life trying desperately to fit into society's thin ideal. Not only that, but I also spent much of it actually helping and encouraging others to do the same. I didn't even know there was another way to look at it until now, or maybe I didn't want to see another perspective.

What I did know was that I didn't want to accept and live the rest of my life fighting to fit in anymore. I didn't want to continue to fight and push my body into looking a certain way. And I certainly did not want to be one of the people who was encouraging it. Pursuing this "thin ideal" had taken a personal toll on me, my health, and my family's life. It wasn't the way I wanted to step into the next chapter of my life…period. I was done.

Grieving Fitness

My life has been consumed with chasing fitness, exercise, and the "thin ideal." And why wouldn't I have? It is all around us. Magazines, TV commercials, and movies helped water the seeds of fat and not being good enough I planted so long ago. I had been part of the problem too. Talking about "burning off last night's dinner" in aerobics class. Telling women how to work out harder or cut back on their food intake. I was a poster child for sharing diets I had tried. I thought I was helping. For over thirty years, I succumbed to diet culture. I bought books, magazines, supplements, diet pills, weight loss programs year after year. Adding my contribution to the $72-billion-a-year diet industry.

Society has become part of the problem. It contributes to letting you know you have a problem. You can't turn anywhere without something or someone telling you how you should look. Doctors add to the problem too by telling you what you should weigh, what you should eat, how you should exercise.

Friends call you and ask you to join the weight loss challenge they are doing at work. They brag to you about the ten pounds they just lost with this new program.

I made the decision to step away from the fitness industry because I realized I was part of the problem. And the problem was, I had no idea where to turn. It had been my whole life. From the early sit-ups in my room, to sports team conditioning to group exercise director. It was all I knew. I had been exercising and teaching exercise almost every day for the past thirty years.

I knew I had to grieve this past identity. It was not all of me, it was only part of me. I had to find other ways I could look at and see health.

I started by disconnecting exercise from burning calories and shrinking or changing the body. I next had to forgive myself for contributing to society's thin ideal and diet culture. By forgiving myself, I was able to widen the lens on how my thoughts were triggering my behaviors. I asked myself this question: What tangible thing could I choose to do or believe that would make the biggest impact right now?

The exhaustion and "doneness" I felt led me to make one of the most important decisions I have ever made. I vowed to myself *"I am officially done with dieting for good."* I am done trying to force my body into a size that it is not, AKA accepting society's "Thin Ideal."

With this one decision, I dove deeply into understanding the physiology of dieting. Of what happens when we try to force the body into losing weight. This research and information were instrumental in starting to change my thinking.

The Minnesota Starvation Experiment that was done in 1944–1945 showed the damaging effects of dieting first-hand. The study was done to research the effects of being in a concentration camp, and the refeeding of prisoners after. They took thirty-six (emotionally and physically healthy) men and cut their essential calories by fifty percent for six months. Here are some of the shifts that happened to the men during this six-month period:

- Their metabolism dropped up to forty percent

- Reduced attention and focus

- Increased emotional distress and depression

- Social withdrawal and isolation

- Increased food cravings

- Constant thinking about food

- Playing with food, rapid eating, over-seasoning of foods

- Increased sensitivity to cold

- Decrease in sexual interest

- Binging and purging

If we knew then that these side effects happen with restriction (dieting), why the heck has it been touted as the best way to lose weight? It took years for the men in the study to recover emotionally and physically.

This study, along with numerous others found in the book *Health at Every Size* by Lindo Bacon, allowed me to see food, eating, and exercise in a new way. I began a new friendship with food and eating while breaking up with my old ideas surrounding exercise.

I also read *Intuitive Eating* (written by Evelyn Tribole and Elyse Resch). This book challenged my beliefs head-on. I was willing to choose to relearn how to trust my body again. I had to tune into my physiological hunger and what my body really wanted and needed. I asked myself, for the first time since I was a kid, how food actually felt when I ate it. Noticed how it tasted and if I really even liked it. I realized how often I was foraging for food when I was not hungry. Looking at food when I was stressed and eating to calm down. Maxi-Me was very busy in the beginning. I had to call on her when I reverted back to the old ways of thinking, and it happened often. I found myself counting and calculating, comparing and criticizing, judging and shaming myself. I had to ask her to be patient, curious, and nonjudgmental all the time.

The fallbacks came frequently at first. A stressful situation with one of the girls, a criticism from work, or a sideways look in the mirror would still lead me to the kitchen. It would lead me to search the internet for a new diet. These stressors found me standing in front of an open cupboard, staring blankly inside. It led me to devour that sleeve of cookies, jar of peanut butter, carton of ice cream, or a bag of chips.

The difference now was how I talked to myself afterward. Instead of hearing Mini-Me's voice come in and give me a harsh verbal lashing, I heard a kinder, softer, more forgiving and genuine voice. This voice would say things like: "It is OK to be sad (angry, frustrated), you're OK, this is painful, you are safe, this feeling will pass, you're human, your mom would find this hard too, she would say 'this too shall pass.'" This one small change helped these episodes diminish.

The sneaking of food, the corners of the brownies, the calculations in my head started to taper off. Day by day, week by week, food became fuel for me to continue to study, write, meditate, or work. The power I had given food slowly began to wear off, and I was beginning to feel free from the prison I was living in.

What worked was to be as open and honest with myself as I could be. Food became more of an experiment. I would think about what I *really* wanted to eat. Something hot, cold, crunchy, soft, spicy, mild, sweet, sour, salty, bland. I visualized how it would taste in my mouth, and how it would feel in my stomach. I asked these simple questions: Would it give me enough energy for what I have coming up in my day? Would it be satisfying? Would it taste good? How would I feel after I ate it? I developed compassionate, nonjudgmental curiosity around eating and food. I released the "good food, bad food" labels

I had placed on foods that were not helpful. I chose to think of food as a friend and ally, not as the enemy.

Triggers

I was quickly tested by my new thoughts around food. It happened on a Tuesday afternoon, as I sat with a friend eating lunch at the 99 Restaurant. It was great to have some time alone with her. She was a longtime client and we had been friends for quite a few years. I enjoyed her company. Just the other day I realized she would be the exact same age as my birth mother. How cool is that?

It had been a great afternoon. I had been present and absorbed in our conversation as I also enjoyed my food. (*Imagine that!*)

Suddenly a harsher tone broke in. It came from within her and invaded this peaceful space.

"Did you just eat all that?" she asked. I could hear the surprise and disappointment in her voice. Instantly I felt sick to my stomach and was fighting off tears. Shame and guilt flooded through my body. One minute I was enjoying conversation and a meal with a friend and the next I wanted to run away and hide.

I nodded. She made a piggy snort with her nose.

Shame storm swirl... "Ya, I shouldn't have," I said as I took a sip of water and dug for my wallet. I had to take a couple more deep breaths in order to fight off the tears of disgust in myself. *She thinks I am a pig.* Mini-Me, there she is, loud and proud in a perfect moment to be seen and heard. *See,* Mini says, *I told you, you have gained weight, I told you, you shouldn't have eaten all that. I told you so, when will you ever learn?*

I had to pause. I closed my eyes briefly and said: Stop! Maxi is in the house now. She spoke up just in time. "Thanks for sharing, Mini, but that is not helpful. Lunch tasted great, you were hungry, this is her stuff, not yours. Take another breath, Anne." The shame started to diminish, and anger began to take over. *She is not me; she doesn't know how hungry or full I am; this is about her, not me. This is her sandbox; I don't have to sit in here and play.*

This woman's words and actions triggered my body into letting me know something wasn't right. This type of trigger used to send me directly to the kitchen, through the drive-thru, out for a punishing workout, or to the store to pick up the next diet book to start tomorrow.

Knowing your triggers arms you with awareness. If I know an experience, a person, or a place might trigger me, I can be prepared. This "Ms. Piggy" experience gave me a new perspective around my body triggers. Triggers are my teachers. The nauseous stomach and the surge of shame are loud signals to pay attention. This experience was something to pay attention to. It became a lesson.

When a surge of feelings (punch in the gut, tightness in the chest, dry throat, nausea, clenched jaw or shoulders, hot, flushed face) came flowing in, I would pause and take a deep breath. This gave me enough space and time to create a speed bump. A speed bump slowed me down. It allowed me to ask some questions. Why did this experience or these words, or that person or that tone of voice, make me feel like crawling right out of my skin? Why did it make me feel less than, shame filled, stupid?

By reframing my triggers as teachers, they became new positive experiences. Whenever I encountered a trigger, it prompted me to stop and pause. It was like a stop sign. Warning, there is something important to notice here! A signal that could help me learn and understand more about myself. I became a student of the trigger.

The teachers became feelings of anxiety, shame, anger, guilt, humiliation, and disgust. They became my body's physical cues of upset stomach, diarrhea, or tightening of the chest. They had difficulty breathing, instant headaches, or flushing of the face. All of these were signs to me to *pay attention* to your thoughts, your feelings, and your environment...**Now.**

Do you know how your body responds physically when it is triggered?

This noticing of my feelings and sequential "speed bump" allowed me to detach myself from my thoughts. I could separate them from me. I have thoughts of feeling smart and stupid, thin and fat, strong and weak all in the same day. So, if that is true, I am not my thoughts; I am only the witness of my thoughts.

Creating a pause and taking deep breaths affords me the time to choose to have a different response. I can shift my thinking with nonjudgmental curiosity. I can ask the questions: What does this moment have to teach me? Why am I feeling like this? What is the story I am telling myself? What do I have control over at this moment? These questions elicit different responses. Instead of falling into guilt, shame, and disgust, I can fall into compassion, gratitude, and growth. We have control over our responses.

As Victor Frankel said, "Between a stimulus and a response, there is a space..." That space allows us to look at the situation and ourselves from a different perspective. It allows us a space to pause and choose a different response (space for a speed bump).

Step Back:

Set a timer for one minute and complete phrases below (a full minute for each one, longer if you would like). Without judgment just write the first things that come to your mind.

1. Food is....

2. Eating is....

3. I get triggered when....

4. What would it look like if you called a truce with food? With your body?

CHAPTER 22

Permission

OUR EMOTIONS (HAPPY, SAD, ANGRY, FRUSTRATED, ANXIOUS, excited, scared, etc.) boil up from inside of us. They get triggered by external events and internal thoughts. Voices, actions, experiences, sounds, words, interactions, memories, and more. These emotions are felt both physically and psychologically. I have found that when we get caught in one of these emotions (like sadness, shame, or anger), it usually gets connected to a few things: one, something that has happened outside of us that triggers a physical sensation or memory; two, the stories we are telling ourselves; and three, the judgment and/or avoidance of the emotion itself (I don't like this feeling, I shouldn't be feeling this way, why can't I get out of this).

An external trigger (words, experience, tone of voice, action) ignites an emotion. "Where are all the cookies?" my daughter asks. Immediately I feel shame, guilt, and anger at myself because I ate them all. This one statement and the feelings that followed would last days and result in either punishing exercise or buying and eating more cookies.

When that same shame and guilt feeling happens now, they last a mere minute or two. This is because I now notice the stories they get caught in and my judgment of them. So, from there I connect curiosity, compassion, and acceptance of them. Now I may say, "I ate them all and they were delicious! I will make some more if you would like."

By allowing the feelings of shame, guilt, and anger in and taking full compassionate responsibility of them, they dissipate. The shame and guilt tend to come from all my thoughts and stories attached to my past. When I am able to be compassionate for my younger self, the result becomes a less intense emotion.

An emotion we allow to be there tends to pass through within a short period of time. The reason it lasts so long much of the time is because of all the stories, experiences, and memories we attach to "said emotion." It usually will include some judgment too. Judgment is connected to phrases like "he is so, she always, why can't he, I am so, I always, I can't, but he betrayed me, but she fired me, yes but I ate the whole cake!"

With a new perspective and the ability to understand and not judge my emotions, I am able to feel them and come out on the other side. I emerge more relaxed and peaceful. "This too shall pass." It becomes the judgment I have placed on the emotion and the stories I may connect with it that makes it last. It is the blaming and shaming of self that makes the feelings hang on so long.

The link between emotions and stress: Fight-Flight-Freeze

One of society's biggest blocks today is stress. We experience it every day. Stress of your life, your home, your work, your body, your health, your family, your circumstances, your past…

Do you know when you are feeling tapped out or stressed? Do you get moody, depressed, anxious, mad, frustrated? Do you get a headache, stomachache, or have difficulty breathing?

Becoming aware of your own individual body's response to stress allows you to identify it and name it. With this knowledge, you can find ways to deal with it.

Most people experience stress in three common ways:

To fight: to make sure your point is heard. This becomes a need to release the energy that has built up inside of you. It comes out through physical, emotional, or verbal release. It is like the way an animal will fight off its predator.

To flight: to run away, to avoid, to hide or to make a statement in a nonverbal or passive-aggressive way. An animal will run away from its predator.

To freeze: To not know what to do or feel, meaning that the emotion gets all jammed up inside of you. This might look like depression, not wanting to get out of bed, hiding from the world. An animal will "play dead" in front of its predator.

By knowing how you react to stress, you become able to experiment with ways to deal with it. You are able to build yourself a stress-response toolbox to help you cope. It is normal to respond differently to stress, depending on where we are and what we are feeling. We have external and internal factors that create either added stress, or less stress.

External stressors can include things happening in your town, state, country, or in the world. They can be linked to how your relationships are doing or how things at work are going.

Internal stressors can include exhaustion, overwhelm, comparison, and worry. Along with anxiety, depression, or increased self-criticism and judgment.

What is interesting is that our old "programmed" thoughts quickly flood into our brains when we are in a stressed-out space and place. We have done it over and over again; it is a well-worn pathway in our brain. That's why it becomes the default choice, and we do what we have always done because "that is just what we do." It has become a habit.

Whenever old thoughts and behaviors came up for me, they were like friends. *Yup, I am stupid…no wonder I binged. I will always be stupid, doesn't matter anyway, might as well eat…* I got swallowed up in a self-deprecating self-talk loop. I sometimes even engaged in a fight with myself, saying, *don't tell me to feel better, I want to feel like this. I can be angry if I want, let me be depressed, let me be sad,* keeping me stuck in old behaviors. Keeping me right there in my uncomfortable thoughts. And for me sometimes this is OK. I allow myself to feel these thoughts.

Other times, the same old behaviors appear due to the fact that I am trying to avoid all those feelings. Somewhere along the way we were told feeling sad, angry, frustrated, or lonely were not good feelings to have. They are undesirable, unacceptable, and weak. This is when I ignore the feeling and stuff it down inside. When this happens, I have just increased the fuel for that particular emotion. This fuel tends to increase the intensity of that emotion the next time it arises.

Handling Uncomfortable Emotions

When we judge our emotions, we act on them accordingly. When I am feeling sad, angry, frustrated, unseen, I look for a way to get out of the feeling. I would much rather ignore it. So, I turn to numbing, medicating, avoiding, and pushing it down.

- I turn to food, even though I am not hungry, to release (flight).

- I turn to alcohol, to avoid conflict and uncomfortable feelings (flight).

- I stomp out of the room to make a statement (flight).

- I become distant and shut down to get attention (freeze).

- I find myself getting swallowed up in social media. I search Dr. Google to find a "fix" or go Amazon shopping (flight).

- I use harsh sarcasm, fighting, or disrespecting whoever is closest to me at the time (fight).

These are my own learned behaviors. My belief, thus my "identity," has been of a runner (flight), one who flees rather than fights or controls. I would numb out and escape into myself. I was my thoughts, I was my emotions, my emotions became me. It was my coping mechanism to think of myself as flawed, inadequate, and substandard. I chose to own these feelings and then beat myself up for feeling them.

Continuing to think of myself this way would keep my life playing out the way it has. Continued numbing, continued lying, continued disappointing. My choice. I could choose another way. So I did. I decided to start sitting with my emotions and feel them. I did this with the help of my therapist. I began the process of allowing myself to feel my emotions without judging them. Yes, you heard that right. I decided to give myself permission to feel. And I allowed myself to *experience* the fullness of the emotion. The most important part was it was done with nonjudgmental curiosity.

The only ways I saw emotions growing up was with the hiding of or expression of the emotion. You either hid your feelings (stuffing them down) or you expressed your feelings. You let everyone around you know exactly what you were feeling. I thought expressing and experiencing emotions were the same thing. What I have come to realize is that they are different. Expression, for me, feels like it is outward. Experiencing feels more inward.

Experiencing an emotion is sitting with it. It is feeling, allowing, and seeing it. Hearing, noticing, accepting, being grateful for it, and loving it. (Yes, no matter what the emotion is.) Experience is a process of permission. Giving yourself permission to feel, without attaching a bunch of stories to it. It takes turning inward toward them and feeling them in the present moment. Letting go of your past stories where you felt the same thing that you want to connect to it.

These stories of our past fuel our feelings. Someone criticizing you brings up feelings of past times you have felt the same way. All the times you have repressed and pushed down shame, sadness, judgment, anger (and more) get attached to the feeling that is happening in the present moment. Whenever we repress an emotion, it doesn't just disappear. It just stays dormant until that same emotion arises again.

I use a backpack analogy. You put a rock in the backpack every time you feel a specific feeling. If every time I have an argument with someone and feel put down, I put a rock in my backpack. After ten years, I will have a pretty heavy backpack. So, when I have an argument and feel put down, my emotion is fueled by all the rocks in the backpack *and* the current experience. This leads to an extremely heightened response and emotion.

"I think we should go over and see if she is OK," I said to my ex-husband, with no response. *"I can't believe he just ignored what I said, he wasn't listening, he never listens. Why can't he see my point of view?"* This one experience became attached to other times I have felt unseen and unheard. My emotion is driven by not only the present event but is elevated due to the stories of the past. It is stored as emotional fuel. *(He never listens to me; he never hears what I am saying.)* And I stomp out of the room and stay angry at him for the rest of the day.

This understanding has given me a new way to handle my emotions. Did you know that according to Dr. Jill Bolte Taylor,[1] our

1 *http://www.drjilltaylor.com/http://www.finding-the-peace.com/2016/10/90-second-emotion-rule*

emotions only last about ninety seconds? As long as we don't attach the emotion to all the other stories or "rocks" we are carrying around.

My mom has always said to me, "This too shall pass." And she is right. Good, bad, or indifferent, all emotions will pass, if we allow them to. The problem is that when we are feeling a "bad" or uncomfortable emotion, we think it is here to stay. That we will never be rid of this emotion, so we stuff it down or try to ignore it. When and if we allow feelings and emotions to move through us and we feel them, they seem to diminish.

Whenever we try to numb them and push them away, we find ourselves swallowed up by them. The more we resist emotion, the more it persists. The more we accept emotions, the more we free ourselves from them.

The Basics

Next time feelings overwhelm you and you find yourself avoiding, numbing, or fighting them, take a deep breath. See if you are able to pause long enough to ask yourself a few questions about where you are right now. This pause becomes a speed bump to check in with yourself. Here are some questions you can ask:

- Are you tired? How have you been sleeping?

- Are you hungry? When did you eat last?

- Have you had any water? Are you hydrated?

- Have you gotten yourself outside lately?

- Have you moved your body?

- When was the last time you smiled or laughed?

Our emotional states are much more fragile when we have neglected these basics. These basics have a big impact on how we respond to what life offers us. If we are low on the basics, we don't have the resources within us to deal with other challenges that may come our way.

After you have taken inventory of your basics, you will notice you may be in a very different place. You have disconnected from the stories that were fueling your emotion. You have reconnected with both your physical self and the present moment. Both these things allow you a chance to take a breath and take a step back to see a different perspective.

Step Back

1. How are your basic needs being met?

2. Do you tend to fight? flight? Or freeze?

3. What triggers you to feel deep emotions?

a. What emotions do you tend to numb, medicate or dismiss?

b. How do you do that (what are your medicators)?

c. What might be a speed bump you can try?

CHAPTER 23

The Gift

THE GIRLS AND I SAT ON THE FLOOR NEXT TO THE CHRISTMAS TREE. It was a year after the divorce and my relationship with them was tenuous at best. I was doing the best I knew how but was still in self-destruction mode. They handed me a present. Excited, I slowly opened it. And staring back at me was the cutest little pink "scary monster" stuffed animal. Her cute pink mouth with the single sharp white tooth. Her tiny pink striped arms and legs and soft stuffed hands.

I started to cry. Happy, wonderful, thankful tears of gratitude, love and joy.

I have named this little stuffed animal Izzy. She came into our lives many years ago during a visit to New York City and the future parents of the babies in my belly. It was Christmas time and the girls and I were visiting the babies' parents. It was a wonderful time to see the city. Shopping, ice skating, and The Rockettes were on the agenda. One morning we took an excursion to FAO Schwarz, the toy store. After waiting in a long line that weaved its way around the building to get in, it was our turn. We entered the massive store in awe.

We had never been in a store so grand. It was more than we could comprehend. Floor after floor, aisle after aisle of toys. All shapes, sizes, colors, textures, types. We were riding up the escalator to the next magical floor when at the top I saw this huge display. There was a fun sign on top saying "Not so Scary Monsters". I ran toward it, feeling like a five-year-old in a candy store because I saw this adorable pink monster. I picked it up and stared at it with a huge smile on my face and turned to show the girls, who were no longer in sight.

I spun around in circles looking for them and spotted them in a section nearby. I started yelling in their direction while holding the little stuffed doll up in the air. *Hmmm, no reaction.* I yelled again and they turned with these faces I will never forget. Heads tilted, eyes saying silently to me, "Mom, geez, get a grip!"

I held tight to the stuffed "monster" and ran over toward them to show them. "Isn't this the cutest thing you have ever seen!" They both nodded, smiled and said, "Ya, sure, Mom, that's really cute, you should get it." Then turned to continue their walk down the Bratz doll aisle. I sighed, smiled, and became sullen all in the same moment. *I can't buy myself something, we don't have enough money. If I spend any money, it needs to be for them.*

I wandered back to the big bin and gently, sadly placed this cute pink monster back into her home.

And right now, she was in my arms. I talked to her immediately and she talked to me back to me in her "Izzy" voice. My heart was full of gratitude. *They remembered. They care, they love me.* I couldn't thank the girls enough. They were both proud of themselves too for pulling this off, and rightly so.

Ms. Izzy has gone everywhere with me. She has traveled and moved five times since then and has landed on the back of the couch I am now sitting on. She has had wonderful conversations with Tim and me. We love her, talk to her and take good care of her. She was even the star of our recent "Pandemic Perspective" Facebook live show.

Every once in a while we take her on car trips with us. She has cheered me on as I ran my first marathon, and she has held on tight to our toll money while she sits on the dash. Due to the fact that she is important to me and was given to me by my daughters, she is well taken care of. She is talked to kindly, appreciated, hugged, smiled at, and deeply loved.

That is what you do with a gift you like, one that you love. You take care of it, you treasure it, you treat it with respect and kindness, in whatever capacity that is. Wonderful gifts are important to us; thus we nurture, take care of, and love them.

So, what happens when you receive a "bad" gift, one you do not care for, from a friend or family member? Usually, these bad gifts don't get shown quite the same love. They may get shoved to the back of the closet. Or they are given away, regifted, or taken to Goodwill or other donation spaces. For most of us, when we like or appreciate something, we take care of it. When we don't, we don't. It is a pretty simple concept.

So, if this statement is true, if I choose to start appreciating and liking my body, might I begin to take better care of it? Might I even nurture it? If we know our actions and behaviors come from our thoughts and feelings, this makes sense. So when the brain receives signals around how you think and feel about things, people, places, and about yourself, it responds. You act accordingly. Your actions are automatic and can even be subconscious. Your behaviors are congruent and instinctual to what you think and how you feel.

My Body, My Business

Izzy helped me realize this. For every one of the five moves I have made since that Christmas morning, she has driven in the front seat. It's because I love her so much that she is treated with such kindness and care. On the last move, I realized how I treated Ms. Izzy. Why have I not ever treated myself like that? I have never thought to like or even appreciate myself. I knew that if I ever wanted to try to treat myself with kindness and respect, I would need a whole lot of help.

I assigned Maxi-Me and her friends to help me. We made the decision to at least stop hating me. Hating my body and hating the choices and decisions I made in the past. I started with a concept called body neutrality. I created a continuum on a piece of paper. On one side was body hate, right where I was. On the other side was body love, something I knew nothing about. In the middle there was body neutrality. I knew I could not jump from where I was to this body love concept. It felt too foreign, too impossible.

But with body neutrality, I was able to at least move away from the body hate end of the continuum. I defined it as the resting place somewhere in the middle where I could move away from the chaos of the thoughts and beliefs I had about my body.

Body neutrality gently quieted the Mini-Me voice. It's a place where I was able to begin the process of body appreciation. I started by being grateful for what my body *could* do at any given moment and disconnected from what it "looked like." Up until this point, I had only ever thought about what my body couldn't do. I focused on what was wrong with it, through comparison, criticism, and judgment. Although I couldn't seem to switch over to really liking my body at the time, I was able to be at least grateful for my body. I was able to step back from the old thoughts with the help of Maxi-Me. I gave her one job. Every day find three things about your body to be grateful for. That was it.

I started with: my legs are strong enough and capable of walking, which allows me to take walks, go to the store, and be independent. My face can smile; when I smile, my body relaxes, and I feel better. My belly gave birth to four children. How amazing is that.

This turned on another switch. The seeds in my brain were getting tilled. I was replanting, refeeding, and refurbishing the way I thought about myself and telling myself a different story. My body is my business. **Your body is your business**, no one else's…period.

Another choice. Choose the old or choose the unknown? The choice to own "no one else is me" period. No one has my unique gene pool, my body type, my personality. No one has lived in my shoes, had my experiences, or lived within my environments. I made the choice to take ownership of all of me.

My body is my business. It is the only one I have and the vehicle that has brought me to this moment. I intentionally began searching to find gratitude and appreciation for my body. I looked back to see all the physical things my body had done for me from a different perspective. The wonder of climbing trees, swimming, skipping, hugging, having children, making sandcastles, or making love. As I stepped into the body neutrality mind-set, I began to develop a deeper acceptance of myself.

Maxi-Me started to speak up more and more. One of her first phrases came from a button I saw at an eating disorder conference: "Not your body, not your business."

The power of this phrase began my journey toward self-respect. It provided me a sense of ownership over my body. I began to listen and trust what my body was trying to tell me. It allowed me to question the tremendous power I had given to others. Even the people closest to me don't know everything about me. I choose not to give others the right to judge me or tell me what I should or shouldn't do. If my body doesn't fit into their perception of "right" or "healthy," that is their business, not mine. This internal conscious choice has changed the way I see everything.

Your body is yours. My body is mine. You get to treat yours the way you want to treat it. No one has the right to tell you how to think, what to eat, what to do, what to believe, or how to behave. Those are your choices.

My body has always taken the brunt of my choices. It internalized all the criticism, judgment, comparison, bullying, guilt, and shame. Society's "Thin Ideal" was God, and Diet Culture was my bible. I believed and consumed it all. All the social bias, the fitting in, the thin ideal, the restriction, and the self-punishment.

When I believed my body did not look like what society said it should look like, I thought of myself as stupid. The way I thought and saw myself was: *"I can't do anything right, I will never be thin, I am a failure"* (my Mini-Me). In other words, I am not OK, not good enough, and not worthy of anything.

For forty years, it is all I have known. The seeds of unworthiness were planted early. Beliefs that my body wasn't good enough took root and dictated my thoughts. So I did what I thought I should do. I tried to fix it. I became stuck in either the "fuck it" mode or the "diet" mode, two roads that are forms of rebellion and punishment of self.

"Fuck it" mode is a rebellious act. It includes reckless behavior, eating whatever you want, sleeping more, and negative self-talk. It also includes numbing behavior (drinking, binging, shopping, etc.), denial, and isolation. This mode is usually followed by huge amounts of guilt and shame, leading you back into dieting mode.

"Diet" mode is a form of punishment. It includes restricted eating, deprivation, compulsive exercise, and lots of degrading self-talk. It also includes guilt, shame, criticism, comparison, and judgment. Along with "should do's" and "shouldn't do's", lots of rules and yeses and nos. Restriction and dieting lead to isolation, emotional instability, and criticism of self and others. This mode can only last so long before your automatic need for autonomy kicks in, and before you know it, you are back in "fuck it" mode.

You have the choice to accept and appreciate this body you are in as your home, the amazing vessel you travel through this life in. OR you can listen to what others think and your own internal network of past stories and past beliefs (of which you have the ability to question). Your choice.

If you don't want to fight with yourself anymore, you can choose to stop. You can be free from the way you have always thought of yourself. You can question your beliefs, question your thoughts, question your behaviors, and question your experiences.

Our seeds were planted from our early experiences. These experiences get attached to specific emotions. From the experience and the emotion our brain interprets the information and then develops and creates an explanation. It does its best to make sense of the experience for you. The explanation an eight-year-old being told they can't have dessert can have many different explanations. What has this eight-year-old experienced in her past? Does everyone else get to have dessert? Is it because she is allergic to an ingredient in the dessert? Are people judging her, looking at her or loving her for wanting dessert? These past experiences play a role in how the child interprets and makes sense of the experience. This explanation (interpretation) will depend on the experiences and emotions she has had in the past (her seeds).

Experience attaches to an *emotion* which attaches to *an explanation.* Because I was called "Annie Fannie Farmer" I felt hurt, sad, rejected and alone. My brain told me it was because I was fat. It was the way I justified the name calling and the explanation I created for myself. It was what made sense to my brain. My interpretation of Annie Fannie Farmer was "I am fat".

By questioning my story, I was able to see my seeds from a different perspective. Maybe the boys in the neighborhood called me Annie Fannie Farmer because I dressed like a boy? Or because I liked to play in the dirt, or wore overalls? Maybe the doctor that year was telling all parents to begin to watch what their kids were eating?

If I had not placed such decisive explanations to my experiences, would I have grown up so obsessed with my body? I will never know. Yet, it does allow me the opportunity to pause and choose to think differently about myself. It allows me the opportunity to look in the mirror with compassion. It allows me the opportunity to thank my experiences because they have led me here to this place and time.

I choose to believe that whatever is happening is meant to happen. We can choose to believe our experiences are happening *to* us or *for* us. Our response is dependent on what we choose to believe. By choosing to sit in resistance to where we are and what is happening, we end up blaming, criticizing, and judging ourselves (or others). By choosing to sit in acceptance of it, we find a way to look at it from a different perspective.

Suffering

What if, from this moment forward, your perspective is that no matter where you are or what is happening, you are where you are supposed to be? What if you are going through exactly what you are supposed to be going through? Through my own uncomfortable and curious experimentation, I found that when I fight what is happening and blame others, feelings of resistance, pain, and suffering actually stay around longer. When I choose to accept what is going on and move with it and allow it, the resistance, pain, and suffering seem to diminish quicker.

Suffering seems to stay with you the longer you fight, deny, and repress it.

Suffering seems to pass through you quicker the more you accept, allow, and feel it.

I believed my pain and sadness were my fault, as was my lack of happiness and joy. It was in the fighting of the pain and sadness and the numbing of it that made it linger longer. The choice to accept pain, sadness, and grief as part of my human experience allows me to appreciate even more the moments of joy and happiness. Life has both, period. And neither lasts forever. They flow in and out like the tides on the beach. The more we are able to ride them, the less they control us.

I have found that if you think and believe people are angry, and the world is an unjust place, that is what you will experience. If you think and believe people are kind and this world is a loving place, you will see the world that way. What you think, you will see. The magnetic spiderweb of your mind will capture the thought and prove to you it is true.

So, if you continue to hate your body, your relationship, your job, or your life, you will continue to punish yourself and beat yourself up. When you criticize, judge, compare, shame, and blame yourself for being who you are, you are treating yourself like a bad gift.

It is easy to turn inward and self-destruct. If you believe you do not deserve love, acceptance, and worthiness, that is what you will see and feel. What choice do you want to make for yourself?

Step Back:

1. How do you feel about your body? Why? (recall your seeds)

2. What is your body story? (look back on your timeline to see if there are any connections to how you feel in your body)

3. What beliefs (seeds) do you have about your body?
   a. How might you see yourself differently? (how might a good friend see you?)
   b. How might you treat yourself like a "good" gift?

CHAPTER 24

Who's Driving?

HAVE YOU EVER BEEN "FOUND OUT" IN A LIE? THE FEELING THAT SITS in the pit of your stomach, making you feel like you want to throw up? For me this feeling quickly calls up my Mini-Me to start beating me up. She is accompanied by my inner attorney (the peanut gallery), who is there to justify my actions. I begin to act in full-on defense mode. Physiologically, this elicits a cortisol spike in our bodies, thus, increasing stress. I become a verbal bully and abuse myself.

Our bodies respond to our own negative self-talk with a stress response. This is because we are being criticized, judged, and even threatened by our own words. We are bullying ourselves. This is what I call controllable stress. There is so much external uncontrollable stress already in our world. Why is it that we still choose to add on more by beating ourselves up?

When Tim found out early on in our relationship that I was drinking in secret, he was disappointed in me. I knew in my heart not only was I drinking, but I was also overexercising and binging too. The minute he found out I was sick to my stomach. I hated myself for it. Mini-Me started up by saying, *You're so stupid, why are you doing this! When will you grow up? You're such a failure.* She was full of negativity, hostility, embarrassment, shame, and guilt. All this hostility was met with the attorney. The justifier. *I can do what I want, you are not the boss of me, if I want to exercise, eat, and drink till the cows come home, I will. So there* (cue hands on hips, sharp pivot turn, and dramatic exit out of the room).

This opposition just continues to add more stress. I end up swimming in a pool of anger and regret. I hate myself for my behavior. For days, I would relive the confrontation and continue to bully and beat myself up over it. Every day I would go through the same verbal assault on myself, over and over. I was in full attack mode of myself every time I thought about it. And I couldn't seem to *not* think about it.

Every time I relived the moment, I brought myself right back there. Then, my body would respond physically the same way it did the moment it happened. Mini-Me popped up and filled me with shame and guilt all over again. I find myself feeling exactly the same, continuing to beat myself down more and more each time. Even though I paid the price once, every time I recall the situation, I pay the price over again. Cortisol spike, stress, self-depreciation, rinse and repeat. I am allowing my Mini-Me to drive the bus of my thoughts and emotions.

Making Assumptions

It is the first day of a four-day workshop. After I try on the fifth pair of pants for the morning, they still feel too tight. There is nothing else to try on, and it is late. I throw up my hands and stomp downstairs. *It doesn't matter, nothing looks good on me anyway.*

The moment I walk into the conference room I look around and wonder what all these people are thinking about me. The "assumption train" has just taken off from the station. I begin to assume everyone in the class has taken one look at me and is talking about how out of place I am. They are thinking how I must be in the wrong place. How I should not be wearing those pants, they are way too tight, *"what was she thinking, poor thing."* Round and round the assumption train goes. Easily and quickly, I allow other people to drive the bus of my inner dialogue.

I continued to make assumptions about what others were thinking. Whatever I was feeling on the inside matched the thoughts I assumed on the outside. I was justifying my own internal feelings of myself. I assumed the worst-case scenario because it connected to and was congruent with what I was thinking and feeling about myself. It was the way my brain proved to me whatever I thought of myself was right.

The truth is unless I straight up ask someone what they think, I actually have no idea what they are thinking.

As a whole, we tend to make assumptions for one of two reasons. One, we make them up to match how we are feeling about ourselves (proving to ourselves we are right); or two, we make them up because we don't fully understand a situation. It is our brain's way of filling in the blanks. We tell ourselves a story (or a few stories) that help us make sense of what is happening.

The assumptions of ourselves and of what others think depend on our own state of mind. If you are in a state of judgment and criticism of yourself, it wouldn't matter what anyone else said to you, or how anyone else looked at you. The stories in your head would be harsh and judgmental. You would hear criticizing assumptions. Your brain proves to yourself you are right.

When you are feeling comfortable and confident with yourself, the assumption train doesn't take off. For example, whenever I put on an outfit I feel comfortable and good in, I don't have those same assumptions. When I am in a space of acceptance of self, self-compassion, or gratitude, assumptions seem to disappear. I could walk into a conference and sit down and Mini-Me would stay sleeping.

My own assumptions around food and my body started early. I would assume others were always watching what I ate or did not eat, if I had gained or lost weight. It was always all about how my body appeared to them. Since I was never satisfied or thought it looked good, I always assumed everyone else thought the same.

Always assuming and giving power to other people's thoughts and opinions. Always feeling judged, never wanting to disappoint and hating the body I had. All I wanted to do was to escape. Because of this, whenever I was feeling less than, I wanted to run away. *Let me live in a cabin in the woods and leave me alone.* These thoughts in my head were continuous. They were always telling me what I should or shouldn't be doing. I continued to be trapped by old thoughts. I wasn't good enough, thin enough, smart enough. Ever. They have kept me assuming everyone else thinks the same. My assumptions drove the bus of my thoughts.

Taking Control of the Thoughts

I have allowed the assumptions of what *I think* others think, along with my own shame and guilt, to be drivers of my bus. My attention seeker (like whenever I lost weight or made a decision so others would notice me) and criticizer have had a turn at the wheel as well. They have all had control of my thoughts and actions.

Mini-Me's thoughts have been in control most of my life. How many people have I let drive my own bus? Way too many to count.

My Mini-Me thoughts have continued to knock me down. They have not been helping me become "better, thinner, smarter." They have been keeping me stuck in the same place. I have been confronted once again with the definition of insanity: "doing the same thing and expecting different results." If I want different outcomes, I must choose different thoughts. There is only one thing I can do: release old thoughts and replace them with others. The only way I can do this is to realize it is possible to change my thoughts. To believe that my thoughts are **not facts**. In order to change a thought, I wanted to figure out the belief pattern it was connected to.

So, when I started to look at my beliefs of not being good enough, thin enough, or smart enough from a different perspective, I was able to notice all the "assumptions" I had been making. I had spent my life connecting the assumptions of what others thought of me to my own thoughts of myself.

So, if I make the choice to send all my Mini-Me thoughts to the back of the bus, who will take the wheel? Who can I count on to help support me in this next chapter of my life?

Maxi-Me and her friends, that's who.

I think about all the voices, thoughts, and people I have allowed to drive my bus. These people have been acquaintances, strangers, and friends. A strange look from a woman walking by has sent me into a self-destructive spiral. The "pumpkin" cop, the piggy nose friend, the doctor's scale, the boys in the neighborhood, the women in the gym, the parents of my daughters' friends. Even the assumptions of my bosses, my coaches, my teachers, my friends. I was always assuming what I thought of me, they were thinking too.

All my assumptions came from my own head. They all came from me. Mini-Me grabbed hold and just made them louder. Did they come from others? I can choose to think yes, or I can choose to think no. My choice.

It is like your assumption train becomes the jury who tells you your fate. It is time to take back control of your own fate, if you choose to. Time to release the assumptions of others. If you want to know what they are thinking or feeling, then just ask. Then, with openness and curiosity, allow them to share with you. With awareness, you have the ability to shift. You first have to notice when you are assuming what others are thinking or feeling. Then make a conscious choice to tell yourself you are assuming. It is at this point you can decide what to do with it.

Who will you let help you navigate your bus? There may be people in your life whose opinions are important to you. Before we go any further...who are they? Who do you trust, value, love, and believe in? These are the people you may want on your bus. You may even allow them to ride shotgun. These are the people you are willing to take some criticism from. These are the only people who have that front seat on the bus and in the story of your life. You get to decide whether they have input privilege...no one else. Period. Your bus, your choice.

New people will come into your life and others will leave. Remember, you are the only one who always has keys to your bus. You have control of who you want riding with you. You decide who has the honor and privilege to support you on your journey. You make these decisions, no one else, not even the person riding shotgun, only you.

If you are the only one driving the bus of your life, what decisions will you make? When you choose to take hold of the wheel to drive your bus, you also get to decide who is there with you. And remember your thoughts drive your bus. Take time to choose your supporting actors and actresses...

Step Back

1. What thoughts or what people do you (or have you) given a lot of your power to that might not deserve it?

2. What assumptions do you make about what they are thinking?

3. Who do you want driving your bus?

4. Who is riding shotgun, and who do you want to travel the distance with you right now?

Who is not here now, but you would like to have a seat on your bus anyway? People who have passed away whose presence gives you peace or strength or confidence?

PART V
FLOURISHING

"*Mother Teresa didn't walk around complaining about her thighs, she had shit to do!*"

—SARAH SILVERMAN

CHAPTER 25

The Body Joyful

Enough was Enough

I didn't seem to care anymore what others thought of me. I now cared about what I thought of me. Continuously trying to be someone else was exhausting. All the checking in and asking myself, who do I need to be for this person? How should I act when I show up for this job? Or when I meet up with this family member or visit this friend? Playing this game has kept my stories and "identities" alive, and I was tired of living them all. I started to think and feel, without judging and comparing myself to everyone else. This has allowed me to show up in this world in a whole new way. MY WAY.

This book is a recap of my journey back to myself. By sitting back and quieting my brain, I was able to listen to important words that showed up for me over and over again. Some of these words were peaceful, playful, kind, caring, compassionate, silly, goofy, lover of nature, animals, and babies. I started to feel like I was living in an old, beat-up, comfortable, and meaningful sweatshirt.

My own nonjudgmental and accepting road map for my space in this world. This was my disconnection from the pursuit of perfection, attention seeking, society's thin ideal, and diet culture.

I have been holding tight to the identities of my past. These old identities at times have been a blessing. My addiction to exercise helped me feel in control when everything around me was out of my control. My addiction to food, restriction, and running gave me something to focus on and be good at. It is OK now to let them go. I have chosen to let them go.

I now seek only things that help me feel light and move away from things that feel heavy. A resurfacing with a different perspective. A relearning of what I like and what I don't, of who I am and want to be. It is both scary and exciting.

There are no trophies for me to win, no badge of approval, no "you're amazing" medal. No cheers, no win-loss record, no easy street. There is also no judgment, no comparison, no regret, no resentment, no perfectionism.

By giving myself this permission to feel deserving, I also allow myself to experience it more. It is on my radar. I am looking for it, seeking it, noticing it, and allowing it (it is my red truck): self-care at its best.

The Body Joyful

Due to the lifelong struggle I've had with my body, food, eating, and exercise, I created The Body Joyful solution. The following chapters outline what I used to heal my relationship with myself. These are the tools that helped me start to think and live differently. I have a positive and respectful relationship with eating, food, exercise, and my body now. Before I was always thinking about calories in and calories out. If I could just control myself to eat less and exercise more, I would be thin and happy. I would like myself. Cruel joke. In reality, every time I was "thin" I still wasn't satisfied, wasn't happy. I was miserable, hated my body, and still felt the need to make changes. My body wasn't the problem; my thoughts and beliefs were.

Becoming aware of where my thoughts and beliefs stemmed from gave me the foundation from which to work. I could see my circumstances differently and shift the way I thought about myself. This gave me permission to question my thoughts and beliefs. A simple shift in thoughts and beliefs, a simple shift in perspective led to completely different results and outcomes. None of this had to do with what I was or was not eating, how much I did or did not exercise, or what the number on the scale said. It was about taking control of my thoughts. It was about searching and seeking for the truth within myself. Owning, forgiving, and accepting myself along with taking full responsibility for my behavior.

In this section, I share with you a more tactical way to see and perceive your own thoughts and beliefs. These are the steps I took for me. What worked for me. Try or experiment with what might work for you and throw out the rest. By sharing this with you, I hope you may find a step or two that can help support you on your journey to food and body freedom. Experiment, collect data on yourself, be open, curious, and aware. *Give yourself permission.*

Since I have recruited my Maxi-Me, my life has taken a one-hundred-eighty-degree turn. I have deeper, more meaningful relationships. I live in purpose and passion. I stumble and fall and get right back up. I learn more and more every day. By accepting all life's ups and downs, I have given myself permission to step fully into them. It has provided me with experiences and memories to treasure. I no longer miss them or say no to them, due to my preoccupation with my body.

Take what you like, leave the rest. Make choices that fit you. Because you are the only you. You're the driver of your bus. The lead of your story. Follow your gut. Be curious, be brave. Step into the story of you, as you are right now.

And Remember!

1. You now know who is driving your bus (your own thoughts, beliefs, worries, and shame). Who would you like to drive your bus?

2. Keep training, inputting, and filling your Maxi-Me daily. She never stops learning.

3. Your body…your business…your perspective. The way you see yourself infiltrates your behavior and outcome. You are a unique and wonderful gift.

4. Your thoughts are not YOU. You have the ability to change them.

5. You can choose to make different choices.

6. Emotions are to be experienced and felt, not judged and hidden.

CHAPTER 26

Identifying Your Values

THE JOURNEY TO LOOKING AT THINGS DIFFERENTLY STARTS BY ASKING different questions. The first few being, what is really important to you? What do you believe in? What do you stand for? These questions aren't as easy as they may look. I had a difficult time with them because I kept answering them in one of three ways. One, my answers were superficial and societal (it is important to be thin). Two, I was making sure my answers would be ones that would make my parents proud, or three, answers that would make Tim proud. I didn't really know what was important to me. I haven't ever even considered it before because I was too focused on what everyone else thought.

Here is the question that began to change everything for me: If you had to pick three values to live your life by, what would they be? What are the three values you want to stand for as you step into this next chapter of your life? To make this exercise a little easier,

James Clear[2] has an easy list that has fifty values to start with. There are sites out there with over three hundred values, which I found too overwhelming, but go for it if you want. Then, take some time to pick your top three.

On my first attempt I circled about fifteen of the words and then broke them down to my top five. Then to three. It is not easy. Think about some of the values you might place in your top ten. Values like family, faith, honesty, contribution, gratitude, autonomy. Or maybe friendships, fairness, growth, kindness, love, peace, service, success, stability.

Take your time and have patience with yourself. This exercise takes curiosity, time, soul searching, and introspection. To narrow it down to only three is hard work. And it's important work.

It's a deep dive into the inner you. Dig below the obvious. Below the values your parents, friends, or colleagues think you "should" have. A good way to tell if you are doing that is if you find yourself justifying or defending a particular value. Take a step back and ask why is this important to me? Whose value might it be? Your mom's? Dad's? Grandfather's?

I was judging my own words and thoughts. Thoughts like, *well that "should" be one of my values, it is important, how could it not be?* Or, *This is a really important value, I should pick it, if I don't what will other people think of me? How could I pick that value? Really? That one is stupid* (Stupid Sally coming for a visit). I kept finding myself picking my parents' values, or a value I admired in someone else, instead of my own. Making this exercise even harder.

2 *https://jamesclear.com/core-values*

Fear may step in. You may find yourself worried or fearful of being judged. Or afraid of not picking the "right" ones or feeling like an imposter. The good news is that these values are not written in stone; try them on, see how they feel. These need to be yours and yours alone. There are no right or wrong ones. Everyone will pick values that might be as different as their DNA.

My one base value is kindness. As I did this exercise, I always fell back to this word. I also continued to judge myself around it. I continued to think it should be something else, something that has more impact, more meaning. I wanted it to be deeper somehow. Yet kindness was the word that always migrated to the top. I made the decision to act, behave, choose, and live with this inside. I want the world to be kinder to one another. I want to be kinder to myself. I would like others to be kinder to themselves. The word "kindness" has a multitude of variations, definitions, and meanings to me.

By narrowing this down for yourself, it makes you think about what the most important things are in your life. I keep my three in mind as I live my life day to day. Narrowing them down is the challenge and the reward.

The Year's Words

A couple years ago, I started a new habit on New Year's Day, instead of the old resolutions. On this first day of the new year, I pick three words to live my year by. My first year it was growth, gratitude, and generosity. The second year it was peace, presence, and play.

This year it is compassion, courage, and contribution. It allows me the opportunity to broaden my value base. (A value may slip into a year too.) The base values continue to be there, yet this allows some flexibility within each year.

It has become another exercise I do with my clients and one of their favorites. These words get combined with their values. It has given them (and me) the opportunity to see things in different ways, due to their focus words. By having some other words top of mind, they may do something they might not have done otherwise.

By picking your words and values to stand by, you can create an ease in the way you live your life. An ease in how you communicate, an ease in relationships. Ease in the way you make choices and decisions and an ease in your work. Because you can refer back to your values and how you want to live your life at any time. Take the time to narrow down what is truly important to YOU…no one else, just you.

The next chapters have "Step Forwards." Take some time here. This section is about you moving forward as you gain more and more wisdom. You will continue to have more experiences that will help you understand more about yourself and why you tend to think the way you do.

Step Forward

1. What are your top three values (what is really important to you)?

2. What three words might you choose to live your year by?

3. How would choosing those words change the way you walk and move through the world?

4. Would it make you stop and think before you say something or act in a specific way? How?

CHAPTER 27

Destination GPS

IF YOU DON'T KNOW WHERE YOU ARE GOING, HOW ARE YOU GOING to know when you get there? For years my only focus was on me. On what I looked like and how others perceived me. Battling with myself to change. To make sure I didn't disappoint anyone. To make sure I looked the way I should and did what I was expected to do. I was always anticipating and assuming what others were thinking or going to think. Constantly turned "on," never letting my guard down and yet I was losing and beginning to drown. It was my husband Tim who asked the question:

If nothing could stand in your way, what would you like to do? To say? To experience? I drew a blank. I had no idea. I was going around and around the same old circle. So, we decided to get away to a small eco-retreat in Maine (a beautiful place called Nurture by Nature) to get real with ourselves. What did we want? Alone and together as a couple. So many of us live our lives on autopilot, with no real destination programmed into our GPS system. This auto-pilot tends to keep taking us around the same circle.

Creating your own GPS helps you drive your bus in a direction that has meaning to you. Here are some of the questions we asked ourselves on that weekend in Maine.

- What do you love?

- What brings a smile to your face and adds joy and happiness to your life?

- How would you want to make a difference?

- Who do you want to impact?

- What do you want to learn to do?

- How do you want to spend your days?

- What things do you want to do?

- What does your perfect day look like?

Knowing what you want to experience, how you want to feel, how you want to live, and how you want to make an impact gives you a GPS to follow. It allows you the opportunity to make some different choices. It allows for new paths, new experiences, new directions.

Whether you have a partner or not, this is an important step in creating the life you want.

If you don't have a road map and don't know where you are going, it is way too easy to fall back into the old stories and old pathways. Our old stories keep us stuck in our old feelings and old behaviors. I am going to be sixty in a few years. I will be sixty and have written a book or I will be sixty and be thinking about writing a book. "I can't go back to school. I will be fifty before I get my degree." I said to myself, "Yes and I will be fifty anyway. With or without a degree."

The most important step I took in redefining the way I live my life was making time to spend with myself. And then some alone time with my partner with only one goal: ask ourselves what we want. I was making the time to identify what I (and we) really wanted. How I (and we) wanted to live. I (and we) identified the relationships we wanted around us and the experiences we wanted to have. Became aware of the feelings I (and we) wanted to feel. We both did the work. I answered the questions for myself, Tim answered for himself, and then we answered them together. It was like we created our own life map Venn Diagram. I did this with him because he is my partner. If you don't have a partner, do it for yourself.

The Destination Postcard

An old client of mine used to send out a wonderful year-end holiday letter. It would contain the adventures of her four-footed friends Timber and Josie and the states that she and her husband had "knocked off" their list. You see, after they had achieved the goal of climbing all New Hampshire's "four-thousand-footers," they became antsy for another goal. They wanted one that involved the two of them and would be exciting and enjoyable to do.

They set their sights on spending at least one night together in each of the fifty states. It would be a fun and interesting way to see the country. So, they posted up a map of the United States in their den and the fun began. At the end of every year, I anticipated the letter she would send. I was able to live vicariously through her journey. This allowed me to see how their goal and vision was being lived: What states had they pinned this year? What adventures did they have in these states?

Taking time to really "see and feel" your next month, six months, or year can be a way of tapping into what is important to you. Being present with your days is key. It is like heading off to the grocery store. You take the same road every time. You get in the car, and before you know it you are there. Hmmm, did I stop at that stop sign? Were there any people out walking today? Our brain checks out of normal everyday activities. It is in these moments where we want to start checking in with ourselves. Time is going to click by no matter what you do with it.

Do you ever wonder where a week or month went when you pause long enough to think back? Isn't it true that more often than not, you can't even remember what you've done? Why not take the time to form intentions and think about what you want to do, feel, or experience? If you don't take time to think about it, the likelihood of you doing, feeling, or experiencing those things will disappear.

There are a couple different ways to do this.

1. Write yourself your own destination postcard, your own end-of-the-year holiday letter. Only write it at the beginning of the year. What adventures did you have this year? Where did you go? You are writing your end-of-the-year holiday letter at the beginning of the year before it even starts, allowing yourself to tell yourself what you did this year. This is a great way to foreshadow your year ahead and to let you know what it is you want to do or accomplish this year.

2. Try talking out events that you have coming up, in the present tense. Talk about how this future event turned out, with embodied excitement and joy. This is a verbal visualization of a planned experience. Before I head out to teach at my retreats, I do this exercise. I talk about how I am feeling on the Monday morning after the retreat, stating out loud how it went. This has helped me release any anxiety, stress, and worry about the upcoming situation. It also helps me enter it with calmness and confidence. It is a verbal way to play out a visualization exercise.

Starting is easy.
1. Pick what it is you want to do, experience, feel, and who might be there with you.

2. Start to talk about already having done it! You can do this into a recorder on a walk out loud (my personal favorite...the ocean, she knows all my visions), or in a journal. Use any of these prompts to help you along.

I remember how...

I remember when...

It was so exciting to...

It felt so amazing when...

3. Allow yourself to keep going, even when you want to stop. The longer you expand, the more interesting your dreams roll out!

Step Forward

1. Where are you headed this coming year?

2. What feelings, experiences, and memories do you want to have?

3. What do you want your obituary to say (I read mine most mornings)?

Taking some time to write your own obituary can be an enlightening experience.

a. How do you want people to remember you?

b. Who is the "real" you?

c. Who will miss you the most?

CHAPTER 28

Defining Healthy

WHAT IS YOUR DEFINITION OF HEALTHY? WHAT DOES HEALTHY FEEL like to you? Defining your personal "healthy" gives you a clearer, more specific GPS. Thinking about what it feels like to be healthy in **your** body creates heightened awareness. What does **your** healthy look and feel like? No one else's. Not your parents', your partner's, or your friends'. Not society's, the physicians', or the government's, just yours. Think sustainable and satisfying. Think energizing and enjoyable.

My choices will be mine. Your choices will be yours. I want to be healthy when it comes to my food choices. My "healthy" means eating chocolate chip cookies. Because when I give myself permission to do so, I don't feel like this food has power over me. I look at food as fun, enjoyable, sustainable energy. As fueling my body. By allowing all foods, I have the ability to listen to what my body is asking for at any given time.

There are no right or wrong and no rules here. This is about respecting and listening to what your body is asking for and needs. As soon as my clients start this process, they take time to ask the question to their body. Once the question is out there, it is surprising what they hear. They listen, they ponder, and then they become able to appreciate all the thoughts that may revolve around it. They realize that their bodies want all kinds of different foods. It is no longer about forbidding certain foods, or "shoulding" themselves around others. It becomes about fuel, energy, pleasure, and taste. How awesome is that? Eating becomes fun again. This one question starts to also affect the way my clients feel in their bodies. They begin to have better relationships with themselves and their families. They begin to step into *their* version of "healthy."

The question to ask yourself is: what does healthy look like to you? Is it feeling a certain way? Is it being able to do specific things? Is it having the energy and confidence to live a robust life? Asking this one question provides an awareness around what habits might help you create this. It provides you with the energy to focus on what is truly important, so you can live a freer and happier life. It is important to realize that your needs deserve to be met. And in order to meet them, your body needs to be fed, moved, rested, and taken care of. When this happens, you can function at your best. You will also understand that when you don't get these things, do these things, make time for these things, everything falls apart. Moods and emotions resort back to the old ways of thinking. This leads straight to old ways of behaving and being. By defining your own "healthy," you start driving your bus. As you do this, I hope you also realize that you are so much more than just the size and shape of your body.

Are you Willing

Wayne Dyer talks about the difference between the morning and afternoon of life. (see resources) When you are in your twenties and thirties, you are in the morning of your life. As you move into your forties, fifties, and beyond, you move into the afternoon of your life. This afternoon of life is a time when you notice different things becoming important. You realize the things that were important in the morning of your life are not as important anymore. In the morning of my life, what was important was thinness, beauty, money, and success. In this afternoon it is kindness, forgiveness, meaning, and purpose.

Willingness to make that one decision to stop dieting for good, and not buy into society's "thin ideal," allowed my life to take a hard right. Taking that turn shifted my relationship with food and my body. I have never been the same. I went from more than ninety percent of my head space filled with counting calories and beating myself up to less than thirty percent. Imagine having twice the amount of time to think and do things that make a difference? Things that impact all the people around you.

This is what intuitive eating has done for me. Pausing long enough to ask the question; what does my body want? And then, even more importantly, trusting the answer and listening. This section of the book is about you asking some similar questions and being willing to answer them, then making some choices for yourself. Identifying what healthy looks and feels like to you gives you direction. Ask yourself the hard questions. Be curious and non-judgmental around the choices. Now, **you do you**.

Being willing is a good way to start.

Here is a manifesto (womanfesto) I wrote for myself:

I am willing to move into the afternoon of life with an open heart. With love, kindness, and compassion. With a space and bubble around me of acceptance, forgiveness, and openness. To share love, laughter, and play with others. To accept myself as I am and others as they are. And always respect myself and those around me.

I am willing to continue to work at owning myself and my story through acceptance, respect, and authenticity. I am willing to be vulnerable. I am willing to continue to learn, so that I may become an impactful, healthy, happy role model. I am willing to treat myself with honesty, love, and kindness and do the things I love. To live a life where I finally let go of what other people think.

I have permission to feel empowered, joyful, and free. I can move, play, and twirl. I can enjoy all foods, I can release expectations, I can feel, cry, laugh, and love. It is the afternoon of my life and I choose to no longer be a prisoner of my own perspective. It is time to set myself free.

And, as God is my higher power, this became my prayer:

Please lead me to become the me you want me to be. The

Annie you had planned for me. Please guide me in the direction you want me to go. I am so blessed to have this beautiful world you created as my playground. You are all I need. I can come to you whenever I am hurting, feeling lost or ashamed, or being someone I don't want to be. Please guide me to be a person you are proud of and that I am proud of.

Step Forward

1. What is important to you as you move into the afternoon of your life?

2. What does it look like for you to value those things?

3. What are you willing to do, to change, to be?

CHAPTER 29

Build a Self-Care Toolbox

WHEN THE PLANE IS GOING DOWN, YOU KNOW YOU SHOULD PUT your oxygen mask on before you help someone else. This is true in life too. If you are not taking care of yourself, you unfortunately can't bring your best self to those around you.

It is easy in today's world to get caught on the "go-go-go-give-give-give" treadmill of life. A place where you are on a continuous emptying of your cup to others, without taking the time to get a refill. I know for me, pausing to take a nap, go for a walk with a friend, or sit and journal was thought of as being selfish. You can't pause a workday to do something like that! Problem is, if we continue to run at the pace we have been, without taking time to refill, we will eventually run out of gas. Get punchy. Tired. Sick. Depressed.

"Self-care" has become a big buzzword, and the term can be completely misunderstood. For many they think it is bubble baths, massages, and manicures. But self-care is more than that. It is about taking a moment to give your body what it might need at any given time. The key to doing this is to actually be aware of *when* you (and your body) are in need of a refill. Not only that, but knowing what kind of care your body and mind need at any given time.

By not listening to the signs of taking care of yourself, you can actually assist in *creating* disease. This can include increased anxiety, worry, and depression. It can include physical pain, illness, and major chaos in your life. Not to leave out pure mental and emotional overwhelm.

The first question to ask yourself is this: How do you know when you need a break? What physical signs (like insomnia, headaches, weight gain, diarrhea, or constipation) show up in your body? What emotional signs (like anxiety, moodiness, isolation, increased sensitivity) show up? Noticing and naming these signs can be an alarm clock for you to know it is time to take care of yourself. These physical and emotional signs let you know you are stressed. Self-care helps to balance the scale. It elicits the relaxation and the rest response (the parasympathetic nervous system, or PNS). This state decreases stress and increases calm.

Most doctors today know how important it is for people to spend more time in this state, this relaxed, calm mental space. It is one of the reasons self-care has become so popular. This being said, knowing when you're in need of a break is important. Being aware that you are either entering into, or in the midst of, your own fight/flight/freeze mode is the key. It is a 9-1-1 call to yourself for the implementation of some self-care.

If you are thinking you're fine and this "self-care thing" is for other people, you are not alone. I spent a year fighting it. I had convinced myself that taking time for me was weak and selfish. *I don't have time for "those kinds of things." Self-care is stupid and can't really make a difference in my life.* It wasn't until I found myself exhausted, completely overwhelmed, and snapping at everyone around me that I decided to pause and take a moment to breath. By doing this, I was able to open my mind and look at self-care from a different perspective.

My self-care journey started by thinking about taking care of my own basic needs. At this point, I was honoring my hunger and respecting my fullness when it came to food and eating. I was beginning to appreciate and respect my body as it was. So, taking care of myself physically made sense. With this in mind, I figured giving myself permission to listen to other things my body might need would make sense too. It was clear that by simply taking care of my physical body, I started to feel better emotionally too. I began to develop my own self-care toolbox, figuring out what works best for me in regards to my own self-care. We all will have needs, thus different toolboxes, different things that can help fill ourselves up. Here are the steps to create yours.

Your Self-Care Toolbox

Step one:

Start by taking out a piece of paper and a pen.

1. Set a timer for three minutes. Brainstorm for the full

three minutes on completing this sentence:
I love to…

2. Reset your timer. Brainstorm on this:
   To relax, I like to…

3. Reset your timer one more time! List as many things as
   you can under this heading:
   Things that make me happy and/or feel good are…

Take your time with this exercise and know that if it is challenging, you are not alone. That is actually the point! We never pause long enough to take time to ask ourselves what we even like.

I recently asked a client, "What do you love?" Instantly her eyes started to water, she looked down at her chest. Life left her body. I held space for her to be in that moment in time because I knew what she was feeling. When she looked up, she shook her head and said, "I have no idea." I let her know she was not alone. I too "had no idea" what I loved and could not think of anything at first. What ended up helping me was when I started to think about my senses. I started imagining all the things I loved to *smell, touch, hear, taste,* and *see.*

For example, I love to listen to the waves in the ocean. I love to admire the colors in the sunrise. I love the feel of my comfy, cozy PJs, and I love the aroma in my kitchen as the coffee brews. So, I asked my client, what smells do you love? What sounds do you love to hear? Her eyes brightened, and she started to write.

Building your own self-care toolbox is an activity that you can do over and over again. Spend some quality time with yourself and think about the questions. Allow yourself to breathe and let's build your toolbox!

Ready? Set? *Go!*

Take a look at everything you've written in the lists above.

1. *Circle* all the things you would be able to do in under five minutes. This might include things like singing a song, playing with your dog, or watching a short You-Tube clip. It could be taking a dance break, snuggling with your significant other, or lighting a candle.

2. Now, *highlight* things you can do in under thirty minutes. Some examples would be journaling, coloring, reading, watching a sitcom, taking a walk. All excellent ways to boost your mood.

3. Put a *star* next to things that take a little more time, things that you love that you can do in about an hour or so. Get outside for a walk, hike, or bike ride. Connect with a friend for a cup of coffee. Meander around a library or bookstore. Watch an HGTV show you love.

4. *Double star* or highlight in a different color the activities that take over an hour. Things like road trips, movies, massages, lunch with a friend, etc.

Create your Box

This can be a fun craft project, or it can be very simple, depending on who you are and what you like. There is no right or wrong way to do this activity. For those of you who want to make this a craft-type project, an idea would be to make four separate containers and label them. You can be as creative as you like when you pick their names. Here is an example.

- The quickie (under five minutes)

- Time-out (thirty minutes)

- Take 60 (under sixty minutes)

- Yee-Haw! (Sixty-plus minutes)

The other way to do this is to simply create yourself a four-box grid. Label each box with one of the four different time frames and proceed to fill it in or fill it up!

Now that you've crafted your self-care toolbox, it's time to start utilizing it.

Here is a starting point for you using your toolbox:

1. The quickie: Engage in these activities on a daily basis. Multiple times a day if you can. Develop a habit to pick one of these whenever you are feeling stressed out.

Dance to your favorite song, text a good friend to let them know you are thinking about them.

2. *Time out*: Most days of the week. What things in your toolbox do you want to engage in to live a more joy-filled life? This is the place for this. I make time almost daily to write in my journal. It fills my soul (finding Joy Pockets in your days).

3. *Take Sixty*: Engage in at least one of these activities weekly. Connecting with a friend for a walk or a cup of coffee, doing a yoga class, or meditating. Spending some time in your garden.

4. *Yee-Haw:* At least once a month. Heading out on a road trip somewhere beautiful. Going to the movies or to a museum. Connecting with an old friend for lunch.

This toolbox gives you permission to engage in activities you love. It allows you the opportunity to feel happy and help you relax on a daily basis. By implementing these activities regularly, you activate the parasympathetic nervous system (PNS). As you already know, this relaxation response decreases stress and increases calm, leading to more joy and happiness.

You are going to be a week older next week, no matter what. Might as well experience more and more "Joy Pockets" (fun pockets, creative pockets, silent pockets) along the way.

When you are in a place of relaxation and contentment, the people around you feel it. You taking care of you creates a ripple effect around you. It impacts others. It gives others permission to do the same. By taking care of you, you become a role model for others to take care of themselves too.

Bonus! This self-care toolbox can be used to help you change your state, anytime you like. Spending time with things that make you happy, smile, or relax shifts your internal energy. When I am feeling sad and yet have to get on a call with a coaching client, I get up and dance to one of my favorite 80s songs. (Thank you, Billy Idol, for the song "Dancing with Myself"!) This instantaneously puts me in a different physical state and frame of mind. It is one of my go to "state changers."

Step Forward

1. What are the signs (both physical and emotional) you have that tell you it is time to take some time for yourself?

2. What might it look like to do something every day that is especially for you?

3. If you were to spend ten minutes every morning (I call this the morning ten) and do something for you, what might you do?

CHAPTER 30

Time to Play

OUR BODIES ARE DESIGNED TO MOVE. THEY THRIVE ON IT. THINK BACK on your childhood for a moment. Do you remember going outside to play? What was that like? What did you like to do? How did you move your body back then? When was it that movement became so hard? When did it become another thing to put on your to-do list?

It was important to me to look at exercise and movement from a different perspective. No matter what your lens is right now on exercise, take a moment to see exercise from at least two other perspectives. You can do this by thinking about a couple of people in your life. How do they see exercise? How has it changed for them over the years? How has it changed for you over the years?

Thing is, we know and have heard about all the benefits of exercise. Society has made sure of it. Exercise helps improve mood, boosts energy, and reduces anxiety and stress. It also increases confidence and improves overall health. Awesome. Does it still make the same impact if it also creates stress, anxiety, judgment, and criticism? If it leads to shame, guilt, and self-flagellation? Probably not. The negative effects of the latter, in my opinion and in my experience, far outweigh the benefits exercise can give us.

The key is finding ways to move our bodies that do not feel like punishment. That do not make us feel weak, not good enough, or guilty. When anything becomes a *should*, or *have to*, it takes on a whole new energy and feeling. We want to find ways to exercise and move our bodies that feel good and don't cause pain. If we find something we like and want to do, we look forward to it and it becomes a more enjoyable and sustainable activity.

My lifelong approach to exercising was to burn off the calories I ate or to punish myself for "cheating" the night before. I spent my whole career buying into what I had learned: more is better, and harder is more effective. I believed if I only exercised long and hard enough, my body size and shape would cooperate with me.

Beat Your Own Drum

The music started and the instructor started clicking her sticks together in the air. She was clicking in time with the music. One, two, three, four… We all joined in; before I knew it, we were moving, clicking, drumming, squatting, and more. I caught a glimpse of my image in the mirror: I was smiling! This was so much fun, I never wanted it to end. Click, hit, click, step. Slow, fast, high, low. *Pure joy.*

My first Drums Alive class. I heard about it at a workshop.

Intrigued, I signed up to take my first class. From that moment on, exercise has never been the same. Drumming started a process that broke apart my whole philosophy around exercise. It replaced it with something much less judgmental and less punishing. The bonus being, because of that, it was much more sustainable!

It was the first time I found myself having fun, laughing, and smiling while exercising! Not *once* did I look at the clock or wonder what my heart rate was. I was fully present and enjoying the experience. *So, this is what exercise should be more about,* I thought.

Up until drumming, I was missing the joy and fun movement and exercise had to offer. This experience brought a wave of new hope, commitment, understanding, and joy for me as well as my clients. The old way of harder, longer, faster was history. I was surprised this new perspective around movement brought me so much peace. For once, moving my body was fun. It was what I needed to take the place of the guilt, shame, anxiety, and worry that was there before. It helped release the hatred and punishment exercise used to be.

I was no longer exercising two to three hours a day with compulsion, dread, and drudgery. I was moving my body in ways I enjoyed. I was enjoying food and treating myself with more kindness and compassion. A single flip of the switch turned on the joy of movement and turned off the punishment and obligation it had grown to be.

Exercise was always a "have to," "need to," "should do," rather than a "want to do" for me. It was more of a chore and a task than a fun activity. This tactic made it less enjoyable and presented all sorts of challenges. It made it hard to get started, to stick with it, and to stay out of pain. By flipping the switch, I found exercise to be quite the opposite. I hunkered down to create a practice of movement that made more sense to me. One that was sustainable, and above all else was fun and enjoyable. The result? What I call the 2x2x2 movement formula.

The 2x2x2 includes releasing numbers (all but the number two!). It lets go of tracking the amount of time or intensity you are "supposed" to do. The 2x2x2 is all about just doing. It includes two days of walking for mobility and independence, two days of play (whatever brings you joy), and two days of functional strength for quality of life. Functional strength is important because it involves movements that help with doing the things you want to do. Like strengthening your legs so you can get up off the floor or increasing your mobility so you can reach the top cabinet in the kitchen.

By moving like this, the body gains all the benefits of exercise. It also keeps your body functioning in a way that allows you to engage in the things you want to be able to do in your life. Like lift babies and animals, play games with children, or walk to the store or mailbox. It helps you to have the ability to reach the top shelf or carry a suitcase or bag of groceries. It is a functional approach to physical health.

Building your Own 2x2x2

Why play? Play is "engaging in an activity for enjoyment and recreation rather than serious or practical purpose," states Dr. Stuart Brown[3] (a play expert). Here's what he shares as the different properties of play:

1. Time spent without purpose.

2. Something you don't want to end (you want to extend the time involved and you lose track of time).

3. A loss in the hyper-sense of self-consciousness (you don't care how you are being perceived by others).

He also shares this notion: "The opposite of play is not work—the opposite of play is depression." According to Dr. Brown, some of the benefits of play include finding joy in movement and trust in self and others. Optimism, creativity, and imagination. Emotional regulation (ability to manage emotions), belonging, connection, and problem solving.

With all of that, why wouldn't we want to play as part of our movement experience! That is why it has an equal part of the 2x2x2! So, what might play look like for you? For me, play looks like throwing a softball around, walking on the beach, jumping the waves, swinging on a swing, or dancing to 80s music.

3 *https://www.playcore.com/drstuartbrown*

Play On

Find activities that speak to you. You can do them alone or with friends; indoors or outdoors. You can do them for five minutes or three hours. Do them for as long as they remain fun and enjoyable. Remember, this has nothing to do with how long, how hard, or how many calories you are burning. It's about moving your body the way it was meant to move. It includes joy, laughter, excitement, and reconnecting with the "I can't wait to go play!" person who lives inside you. It also involves being grateful to your body for what it can do. Playing is all about being open-minded, curious, nonjudgmental, and thinking outside the box. What follows may sound like fun. It may sound like it's just for kids, and it may even sound like everyday, ordinary activity.

Some examples of play might include biking, skipping, and galloping. Swimming, kayaking, playing hopscotch, or roller-blading. Mall or museum walking, dancing (alone, with friends, in celebration), or drumming. Play may be going to a playground with kids, kicking or throwing a ball around. It could even be one of my personal favorites: foot golf (a soccer and golf combo)!

Play also includes many environments. Think about some of the places you like to go to. Might there be movement involved there? Maybe it is heading out to find playgrounds or parks. Beaches, ponds, pools, fields, tennis courts, malls, hills, mountains, and trails. The list is endless. Maybe it involves asking friends or family members to join you.

To get started, list and experiment with lots of different ways to move your body and start walking. That's it. Getting the body moving in this way gives you permission to enjoy it, with less pressure and judgment. Remember, no time limits. You can start with a three-minute walk around your house. No rules. No right or wrong.

Step Forward

1. What beliefs about excercise do you hold onto that may be holding you back from enjoying it?

2. What type of play are you willing to experiment with and try?

3. What types of movement *feel* good in *your* body? (Add these!)

4. What movements and exercises don't feel good in your body? (Let go of these.)

CHAPTER 31

Cultivate Your Environment

HAVE YOU EVER CRIED BECAUSE A FRIEND WAS CRYING, HURT BECAUSE your child was hurting, or laughed because the room was laughing? It's interesting how we take on the energy of what is around us much of the time. It is actually a scientific response. We have something called "mirror neuron" brain cells. They trigger us to mirror the feelings or responses of others. With this in mind, we might want to consider who we spend a great deal of time with.

Jim Rohn[4] says that "we are the average of the five people we spend the most time with." Take a moment to wrap your life around that statement. Who do you spend most of your time with? When I first heard this statement, it was near the end of my first marriage. I decided to take a closer look at the people who surrounded me. It was enlightening. What I found was on one hand comforting, and on the other, frightening.

4 *https://www.businessinsider.com/jim-rohn-youre-the-average-of-the-five-people-you-spend-the-most-time-with-2012*

I had some wonderful people who inspired me, cared about me, and were kind and supportive of me. So, I sat down at work one morning, in the quiet calm of the gym before it opened. I started to list this group of people and proceeded to write down the common traits they brought into my life. These were some of the traits that I identified:

Caring, kind, and compassionate
Nonjudgmental
Dedicated
Encouraging
Open
Curious
Supportive
Lighthearted, fun, funny
Carefree/playful
Giving
Grateful

Then, I looked at some of the other people in my life I spent a lot of time with, and I listed their traits. There were some of the above words, plus there were these:

Judgmental
Opinionated
Stubborn
Self-serving

Sarcastic

Negative

Complaining

Pessimistic

I took my own step back. At first, I saw this second list as all negative. I saw it that way because it was what I wanted to see. Within minutes, Mini-Me started up. She started with her judgment and criticism of my choices. I put on my sneakers and went out for an early morning walk, list in hand, hoping I might quiet her down. I was walking, in tears, questioning why I had made the decisions I had made. How could I have not seen these traits? How I could I have been so stupid?

After ten minutes of tears and self-flagellating, Mini-Me took a break. It was in that pause, I lifted the list to look at it again, but this time with a different perspective. I was able to see that these traits could also be seen as great ones when used in the right circumstances. It can be very helpful to hold true and strong to an opinion sometimes (much of the time actually). I quite admire it. It can also serve you well to be stubborn over something or complain about something. It can make a real impact.

The fact was, while I was living in it, I was unable to see it this way. I saw these all as negative and allowed them to infiltrate my soul in a way that was harmful to me. I *allowed myself* to feel angry, negative, opinionated, and sarcastic whenever the people with these traits were around.

I would say they *made* me feel stupid, unworthy, fat, ugly, selfish. *They* judged me, *they* were negative and unsupportive. *They made me* feel bad about myself. There were two reasons why I thought this. One: I was feeling this same way about myself, and two, I wanted to feel that way. I blamed my environment.

Once I started to look at all people with a different perspective, I realized I had gotten good at blaming others for the way I was feeling about myself. Instead of taking responsibility myself, I was blaming them. It's so much easier to blame someone else for the way you feel. It's much harder to take responsibility for your own thoughts, feelings, beliefs, behaviors, and actions.

I built up a wall around me that became thicker, higher, and stronger every day. I shut myself down, put my wall up, and made damn sure nothing was going to get to me. I brought into my relationships all my own "not so great" qualities. When I was with someone who was judgmental, I became the same. When I was around others who were having a complaint party, I joined right in. Stubborn? Yup, I can do that. Sarcastic? Yup, got that covered too. I would mirror whoever I was with. So, the statement about becoming the average of the people we hang around with is all too true for me. I was the chameleon of personality.

When two similar types of negative energy meet with different agendas, there is not much chance of getting along. Each person most likely will have a hard time hearing the other… unless they are both open and willing to take responsibility for their own stuff. I didn't understand this, so I spent an enormous amount of time and energy in blame and protection mode. It was my default over taking responsibility and understanding myself. In turn, the environment I created was much more negative for everyone within earshot. Unfortunately, this negatively impacted the most important people in my life: my girls.

Now that I understand and realize this, I have the ability to choose who I spend time with (for the most part). I have created my own "circle of influence." I choose to surround myself with people who have the energy I want to be around. People who support me, inspire me, challenge me. People who model the behaviors I want to have. People who will continue to make me a better person. (This circle includes all my clients—I make sure of it!)

I look at this circle of influence like a seesaw. On one side, there are the people in your life you really love to be around, who support you and give you energy. On the other side there are people who may judge or criticize you or may be self-centered or sarcastic. Or people who may be more negative and unsupportive. We all have people like this in our lives and we love them too. They teach us things and give us different perspectives to think about. And there are many people in our lives who have both sets of qualities.

So, what can we do? Especially about the people who may impact us negatively, yet we still want to keep them in our lives.

Like a parent, a child, or a boss. How can we positively impact our own living environment?

Create a Self-Care Sandwich

We sometimes face spending time with people who are hard and who we don't really feel good around. Even people we dread seeing and spending time with. In these kinds of situations, there are some things that we can do to help protect ourselves.

1. Limit the time we spend with them.

   Are there ways that you can set up boundaries around the time that you spend with these people? I talk to my clients about making sure they are proactive around the time they spend here. They let the person know ahead of time that they have an appointment and have to leave after an hour. Or they may set a timer for fifteen to twenty minutes when they talk with them on the phone. They also may decide to spend time with them in a place where the contact with each other is minimal (go to a movie, concert, game, or show with them).

2. Sandwich yourself with self-care...

   Make sure you go into these interactions with your cup filled. This becomes one half of the sandwich. If you have your own cup filled, it becomes easier to be in the presence of someone who might drain it. The other half of the sandwich is to make sure you have something on the other side of your time with the person to fill you back up. It might be a dinner with a friend whom you love to be around. It may be taking a bath, going to the park, or watching your favorite movie. Think about what makes you happy and brings you joy. Sandwich these things on either side of the time with this person

3. Be open and honest with yourself on who you are when you are with this person.

    In other words, who do you bring to the table? For me, I knew I was completely armored up. Meaning I brought my own sarcastic, negative, "walls up" energy with me into all interactions. I was already in fight mode before I even walked through the door. What came next was inevitable. I realize now, if I was able to bring the kind and compassionate part of myself, things may have been different. Do I know that for sure? Not really, but I also don't know the latter. So, I am now intentional on how I show up in any given situation. A great example of this comes from Oprah. She has a sign over her office door that reads: "You are responsible for the energy you bring into this room." Bravo.

Building your Team

If you are the average of the five people you spend the most time with right now, do you like the odds? Who do you spend the most time with in your day-to-day life? Do they support you? Encourage you? Challenge you? Love you unconditionally? Are they negative or positive? Do they have similar values? Do you feel good when you are with them? Or do they drain your energy? Do you feel bad about yourself or shameful when you are around them?

You have the ability to build your own circle of influence.

Step Forward

1. What does your seesaw look like?
   a. The goal here isn't to have one side loaded and nothing on the other side. The goal is to tilt the seesaw a little more toward the supportive and positive side.

2. Who do you really enjoy being around? Are you able to be around them more?
   a. Some tips: Ask! Plan, call, email…make time.

3. Who is harder to be around? Are you able to reduce the amount of time you spend in their presence?

CHAPTER 32

Harvesting Happy

THIS BOOK HAS BEEN ABOUT MY OWN JOURNEY. ME, SHARING A LIFE full of dieting, restricting, drinking, and overexercising. Full of people-pleasing, numbing, obsessing, and comforting myself. It is about making mistakes, trying to be someone else, and then judging myself for it.

It is a story of being stuck in a self-made version of *Groundhog Day*, until one day I woke up and was sick of it all. It is the journey I took from the day I woke up sick and tired of playing the weight loss and self-hatred game. Sick and tired of playing the "when I....then I..." game. (When I get thin, then I will be happy. When I lose ten pounds, then I will go to the beach.) I didn't want to play anymore, I was tired of always losing. I didn't want to diet anymore. I didn't want to exercise for time and calorie burn anymore. I didn't want to beat myself up anymore.

I made a critical and difficult choice to step out of living in my version of *Groundhog Day* and playing the "when I....then I..." game. It was important for me to realize I was worth living in an environment of peace. In a place where I didn't feel like I had to be someone else all the time and had to "walk on eggshells" to keep the peace. I decided to get a divorce. It was one of the toughest and most heart-wrenching decisions I ever made. I was so fearful of hurting others—ok...terrified of hurting my children and my ex. The thing is? When you make a decision like this, you *do* hurt others, and I did. And I am so very sorry for that. I disappointed important people in my life. It was not the first time, nor will it be the last. In my gut, I knew this was the right decision. Even with the circumstances I could see before me.

Here is something interesting I found out. Every time you make a decision with foreseen circumstances, they contain unseen circumstances too. By honoring and respecting myself through this decision, I was able to be there for my girls in a whole new way. If I had stayed, I would have demolished my marriage, damaged my daughters even more, and drowned myself. I feel as though I became a better mom, and the girls' dad, I truly believe, became a better dad. But you would have to ask the girls about those assumptions.

The choice to step out of this game I was in was a sign from the outside. It was when my identity slowly deconstructed and disintegrated in front of me. This choice came from the loud, sharp, constant pain that radiated from my left knee. Day after day, step after step. It screamed at me it was done. *Please stop! Please...stop...*

As I sat in that hospital and realized I was not going to be able to get the surgery I wanted, I had to pause. I chose to ask heart-awakening, difficult questions. My emotion was stuck in high gear. I was angry, frustrated, hungry, and tired, so these hard questions came roaring in. "What are you doing? Why do you keep putting yourself in these positions? What was this surgery *really* going to do? Help you keep self-destructing? Is this the way you want to keep living?"

I was exhausted from running on this hamster wheel going nowhere. And since my knee was too bad to get that one surgery, I ended up with a full-blown knee replacement at fifty years old. During my rehab time after this surgery, I took an even closer look at the life I had been living.

I realized I had spent my whole life trying to prove to myself, along with everyone else, I was worth being here. I was worth being born. I had been looking at things in my life with a pair of singularly focused glasses on. Seeing only one perspective. This perspective had kept me trapped and imprisoned in my own mind, body, and life. I have missed out way too many moments and memories. It was time to call a truce and form a new relationship with myself and my body.

My perspective was blurred by the seeds I planted in my childhood. I interpreted my experiences in very specific ways. Because of this, specific seeds of thought grew. These thoughts found proof wherever they looked. They had been trained to look for it. I owned and strengthened my own story by continuing to believe everything I thought. I sought out acceptance and worth from outside of myself. And listened to the bullies in my head. I also believed my thoughts were the only thoughts available to me. By looking at my life with that singularly focused pair of glasses, I was only seeing one perspective.

When I looked at my life through another set of glasses (another perspective), my vision changed. I was able to see the destruction and devastation I had created through my own thoughts. I was able to now own my behaviors, by taking responsibility of them. I chose to forgive myself for the decisions I had made. Forgive myself by the way I treated myself. I knew that if I didn't, I would stay running on the hamster wheel. I chose to start treating myself with kindness, respect, and compassion. I asked for help and support to help me make different choices. I found my way out and have changed the trajectory of my life. I eat, move, think, interact, play, choose, feel, notice, and respond differently now.

As part of this journey, I took the time to become appreciative of every part of me. I was able to step away from the old chorus of voices in my head (my Mini-Me's) and truly embody and hear my new Maxi-Me team. As part of my healing, my Maxi-Me team and I made a list of the things I am now grateful for about my body. Being grateful for what my body can do vs. what it can't do allows for acceptance and respect to flourish. I no longer take my body for granted. Here is my body list with my new perspective. I encourage you to make a similar list.

- My feet love to splash in the water...in the ocean, in a puddle, in a lake or a stream.

- My legs love to feel the warmth and softness of colored leggings. They love to walk, anywhere and everywhere, the beach, park, trail, mountain, mall, sidewalk.

- My hips like to swing a hula hoop from side to side.

- My stomach loves to laugh so hard it hurts.

- My lower back loves to feel the loving touch of my husband's hand as he walks with me.

- My chest enjoys a nice deep breath of cool fresh autumn air.

- My arms love to hug…family, friends, animals, and trees.

- My hands like to write and color with crayons.

- My fingernails love the chance to be French.

- My upper back loves a deep-tissue massage.

- My neck enjoys the rainbow of turtleneck colors I wear.

- My mouth loves to share a smile.

- My tongue enjoys the taste of so many different foods.

- My nose loves the smell of fresh-cut grass, coffee brewing in the kitchen, and the scent of a blooming lilac tree (my mom's favorite).

- My ears love the sounds of waves crashing on the beach, wind chimes on the deck, and the voices of my daughters on the phone.

- My hair enjoys the freedom to do whatever it wants every single day!

- And my eyes? Well, they are blessed to see the world with a different perspective now. Instead of them traveling directly to the places on my body I used to hate, they see something completely different.

We are all so much more than the size and shape of our bodies. These bodies of ours can see and feel love, light, joy, and strength. They are uniquely talented, passionate, determined, and gifted. They are compassionate, caring, kind, forgiving, and grateful. These thoughts were available to me years ago. I just didn't know I had the choice or the ability to give myself permission to think about them, much less choose them. The difference is, I now know they exist, and I have made a conscious choice to put my focus and attention on them. Where I had been putting my focus for the last forty-plus years was not working anymore. I took a chance to look at a different, scary, and unknown perspective.

I encourage you to do the same. Take a step back, take off those glasses you have had on for so long and look around. Give yourself the opportunity and the permission to see a different perspective. The awareness that there is another way to see things can open the door for you to freedom, peace and joy. As my clients start to see different perspectives, they have begun to see and feel their lives change.

As the great Wayne Dyer said: "When you change the way you look at things, the things you look at change."

CHAPTER 33

The Body Joyful Cliff Notes

-Your body is a vehicle that moves through this world. It gets you from point A to point B. It can listen, speak, and voice an opinion. It can, if you choose, be a life-changing vessel.

-Your body is amazing. Everything can change once you give yourself permission to listen to it, feed it, fuel it, enjoy it.

-If you continue to see your body and worth with your past emotions, experiences, and feelings attached, nothing changes.

-You are the writer and author of your next chapter. This is your story to write from here. What experiences, people, memories, and impact are you going to write about and experience?

-You have the ability to comfort others and make others laugh. You can impact them with your stories, words, experiences, songs, ideas, love, passion, work, and more.

The solution is simple (yet not easy). It starts by looking at five parts of your life from a different perspective. Your thoughts, yourself, your body, food, and exercise. This is not a prescription. This is just what worked for me. My hope is there may be something on this list that might help you too. Then ask the question: What one thing might you be willing to try to see if it works for you?

1. *Shift your inner dialogue and self-talk.*
    a. Be kind and compassionate to yourself.
    b. Forgive yourself. You did the best you could with what you knew.
    c. Become grateful for who and where you are right now.
    d. Recruit a new neighborhood in your head with voices and thoughts that will help to strengthen and support you.

Notice, appreciate, and move to the back of the bus (or into another neighborhood) the negative, self-sabotaging voices. They have created superhighways in your brain. It is time to recruit some new compassionate, positive, and encouraging voices. They can help create new pathways and superhighways. NOTE: Our hope is that the older negative superhighways become more like back roads that don't get as much use anymore.

2. *Take care of yourself, make sure to fill your cup.*
    1. Sleep and rest (lack of sleep can affect *everything*! Make sure to give yourself permission to rest).

2. Move your body (in whatever ways feels good to you).

3. Breathe, meditate, journal (tap into your parasympathetic nervous system).

4. Fuel yourself with foods that taste and feel good in your body.

5. Connect with people who energize you and lift you up.

6. Find fun wherever and whenever you can.

7. Laugh out loud.

8. Step outside, absorb and check out the beauty of nature.

9. Discover your joy, whatever it is that makes you smile and lose yourself, for this is your purpose. Find yourself daily Joy Pockets (and then enjoy them!).

10. Develop a gratitude practice.

Taking care of yourself is like putting the oxygen mask on before you help someone else. We know that trying to quench your thirst by drinking from an empty cup doesn't work. Fill your cup; it benefits everyone around you.

3. *Begin the journey toward acceptance and appreciation* of your here-and-now body.

 1. Focus on what your body can do instead of what it can't.

 2. Be grateful for your body for it is the only vessel you travel this earth in.

3. Make a list of all the nonphysical qualities and traits that make you who you are.

4. Forgive yourself.

5. Give yourself permission to grieve the way your body used to move or be.

6. Make the *choice* to think of your body is a *good* gift.

When you focus on self-hatred, your behaviors and life will mirror those thoughts. You will continue to punish yourself, beat yourself up, numb, and medicate. And in ten years, you will be doing the same. When you focus on appreciation and acceptance, your behaviors follow your lead. You will nourish, pause, play, give back, share, and make a difference.

4. *Eat intuitively.* (*Intuitive Eating* by Evelyn Tribole and Elyse Resch)

1. Listen to your body and ask it what it needs.

2. Develop trust between you and your body (beginning to trust what your body says and being patient with your body, as it learns to trust you).

3. Tap into and discover your body's internal hunger and fullness cues.

4. Eat when your body is hungry and stop when it is full.

5. Eat what your body wants to eat, and you know will satisfy you.

6. Quiet down the inner food police (your Mini-Me).

7. Remember that only you know *you.* No one else

knows any better than you what you need.

5. *Play!* Move your body in ways that feel good to you. Dance, walk, twirl, drum, lift weights, box, stretch, do yoga, ride a bike, swim. Your body is designed to move. Find something that is yours. Something you like and that feels good to you. If you enjoy it, it becomes a "want to," not a "have to," thus becoming a new part of who you are.

Give yourself permission to experiment. What if exercise could be totally different? What if it could be more like play? Like playing hopscotch, swinging on a swing, or gathering shells. What if it could be walking more by parking farther away? Continue to ask yourself how do some of these things feel in your body?

My past has led me to my purpose. My experiences and the way I interpreted them has kept me in prison. It was within this prison, I found myself unhappy, addicted, and stuck. I had created well-worn paths, going round and round. The awareness I was in there, being held by my own free will of my perspective, gave me the key. This prison eventually led me to peace.

It is now my mission to help women heal and recover from diet culture and society's "Thin Ideal." So young girls and teens have positive role models who know their value and true worth, regardless of what the scale says, or what size or shape society's ideal tells them they should be.

By starting the journey to see yourself differently, you will make a special one-of-a-kind impact on this world. You become a role model for our next generation. And you will cause a ripple effect because you chose to share your authentic self with those you love.

The Body Joyful!

If you are interested in starting your own Body Joyful journey, join the *Body Joyful Revolution Community*. This is a non-diet space that contains free content and offers support and strategies to become a Body Joyful Woman.

Our mission is to guide thousands of women regardless of size, shape, or weight to feel more comfortable and confident in their bodies and selves so they can know their true value and worth.

A Body Joyful Woman says no to diets and rejects society's "Thin Ideal" and is a powerful role model for helping future generations to do the same.

The Body Joyful Revolution strives to reduce bullying, weight stigmatization, and body shaming, decrease the number of disordered eaters, and help prevent life-threatening eating disorders.

We would love for you to come join us and help us make the world a little bit better!

https://www.facebook.com/groups/bodyjoyfulrevolution. And consider purchasing a book for a friend, coworker, family member, or your entire organization. It is time to change the conversation and change the trajectory of our next generation.

APPENDIX I. RESOURCES

The following is a list of the coaches, mentors, authors, and instructors that are talked about or stated in the book. It is a partial list of the people who provided me with insight, understanding, and knowledge as I traveled through my healing journey. For a more comprehensive list, visit me at The Body Joyful Revolution on Facebook or contact annepoirier11@gmail.com

Kyle Cease https://kylecease.com/

Byron Katie https://thework.com/

Brené Brown *The Gifts of Imperfection: Let Go of Who You Think You're Supposed to Be and Embrace Who You Are* (paperback – August 27, 2010, Hazelden Publishing; 1st edition)

Dr. Shad Helmstetter https://shadhelmstetter.com/

Minnesota Starvation Experiment https://eatingdisorders.duke-health.org/education/resources/starvation-experiment

Lindo Bacon. *Health at Every Size: The surprising truth about your weight* (October 11, 2008, BenBella Books)

Evelyn Tribole, Elyse Resch *Intuitive Eating* (September 11, 2003, St. Martin's Griffin)

Wayne Dyer https://www.drwaynedyer.com/ *The Shift: Ambition to Meaning: Finding Your Life's Purpose* (2009, not rated)

James Clear https://jamesclear.com/

Nurture through Nature http://www.ntnretreats.com/

Drums Alive https://www.drums-alive.com/

Stewart Brown https://www.playcore.com/drstuartbrown/

Jim Rohn https://www.jimrohn.com/

ACKNOWLEDGMENTS

This is the part of the book I most look forward to and most dread. How do you put into words appreciation that is felt right down to your toes? Every person who has entered and exited the story of my life has taught me something. I am so very grateful for each and every one of them.

I have to start with my wonderful, supportive, encouraging husband, Tim. He came into my life in a time where I was feeling lost, fragile, and broken. His love and support have been the glue that put me back together again. He has encouraged me, challenged me, and celebrated me. He helped to rebuild my foundation. I am eternally grateful for him.

To my daughters, Alyssa and Ashley, what can I say? I hope this book shows you that anything is possible. I hope it lets you know how much I love you and how much I believe in you. My biggest hope is that my journey helps and empowers you both to step fully into yours. You have proven to yourselves your strength, resilience, compassion, talent, dedication, and independence. May you both step into your stories and write ones that make you happy.

This book is dedicated to my parents. They took me in and gave me a loving and supportive home. They pushed me to be hardworking, dedicated, caring, and strong. My mom passed away during the writing of this book. I know she is looking down on me, cheering me on. It was her grit that pulled me out of a downward spiral as a teen. My dad to this day is one of my biggest fans. He has instilled resistance and perseverance within me. He taught me how to throw a softball, kick a soccer ball, shoot a basket, and walk on stilts, picking me up whenever I fell. Thank you both for your love.

To my in-laws, Jackie and Wendell. I wrote some of this book at their camp in Maine, looking out at the water. They accepted me into their family like I was their own, sharing with me their love, grace, and faith. Their support and encouragement have been invaluable to me.

To my birth mom. For her courage to say yes to adoption instead of abortion, to say yes to pregnancy and giving me life. Without her grit and tenacity there is none of this. No book, no children, no family, and a completely different life for all involved in the story of my life.

To my therapists, mentors, coaches, colleagues, and friends, thank you for your support. For your guidance, consistent encouragement, and for holding me accountable for my actions.

Coach Dave Garcia, thank you for being my compass, always directing back into my true north. Pam, Dawn, and Karen, you have always been there for me to listen, encourage, and lift me up when I couldn't do it for myself. Cheryl and La, you are my rocks. Thank you all for extending your loving hand to me over and over again, never giving up on me.

To the obscure connection and love of Ken and Maria in finding Nancy Aronie. It was Nancy's workshop, "Jump-start Your Memoir: Writing from Your Heart," that was the catalyst for writing this book. It was her compassionate circle of writers that actually helped me realize I had something to say. I will forever be grateful to her. To her amazing community and her belief, support, and encouragement.

To my amazing clients and members of the Body Joyful Revolution. You continue to inspire me to be better, to do better. You teach me vulnerability, belonging, compassion, grace, acceptance, and appreciation. We challenge each other and learn from one another. I am so very grateful to be a part of this community.

And finally, to God for his forgiveness and for his relentless, unconditional love. For the beauty he has created in this world. I count on his sunrises, sunsets, rainbows, and snowstorms to keep me grounded, humble, and grateful.

About The Author

After struggling with her own weight and food issues, negative self-talk, and poor body image, Anne was inspired to leave behind society's thin ideal and say no to diets for good. So, she set out on a journey to find a more compassionate, self-accepting way to live. Her mission is to empower and support other women, regardless of size, weight, or shape, to feel comfortable and confident in their bodies and selves. Anne is a certified intuitive eating and body confidence coach, play and movement specialist, and self-talk trainer.

Other online publications featuring her work include *Eating Well* Magazine, *Huffington Post*, *Living Well*, *The Guardian*, *Body & Soul*, *The Cut*, and others. Anne has two adult daughters and lives in Old Orchard Beach, Maine with her husband, Tim. She is a lifelong learner and loves walks on the beach and taking pictures of sunrises along the coast.

Made in the USA
Las Vegas, NV
07 October 2022

56688623R00187